For Beginners LLC
62 East Starrs Plain Road
Danbury, CT 06810 USA
www.forbeginnersbooks.com

Text Copyright: © 1992 Richard Osborne
Illustration Copyright: © 1992 Ralph Edney
Cover Design: Renée Michaels
Supplemental Typography and Production: Sam Moore/Windhorse Studio

A For Beginners® Documentary Comic Book
Originally published by Writers and Readers, Inc.
Copyright © 1992

Cataloging-in-publication information is available from the Library of Congress.

ISBN-10 # 1-934389-02-1 Trade
ISBN-13 # 978-1-934389-02-7 Trade

Manufactured in the United States of America

For Beginners® and Beginners Documentary Comic Books® are published
by For Beginners LLC.

Reprint Edition

PHILOSOPHY

FOR BEGINNERS

by Richard Osborne

Illustrated by Ralph Edney

Table of Contents

W HY DOES PHILOSOPHY GIVE SOME PEOPLE A HEADACHE, OTHERS A REAL BUZZ, AND YET OTHERS A FEELING THAT IT IS **SUBVERSIVE & DANGEROUS** ?

W HY DO A LOT OF PEOPLE THINK PHILOSOPHY IS TOTALLY **IRRELEVANT** ?

W HAT *IS* PHILOSOPHY ANYWAY ?

How can you recognise a philosopher in the street?

We'll try to answer **some** of these questions

Some philosophers will naturally argue that looking at the general history of philosophy is an impossible, possibly distorting, task — but as one philosopher said, it's better to do evil than to do nothing.

WHY DOES BEER TASTE BETTER AFTER A HARD DAY'S WORK?

I DUNNO—I'M NOT A PHILOSOPHER

SO WHAT IS PHILOSOPHY? SINCE NO ONE AGREES, IT'S PROBABLY THE WRONG QUESTION TO START WITH — BUT THEN MOST PHILOSOPHY STARTS WITH

THE **WRONG QUESTION** OR THE **WRONG ANSWER**

In Greek, philosophy means the 'love of wisdom' which seems like a reasonable definition, but doesn't get us very far, since there have been very sharp disagreements about 'wisdom' throughout history

RIP
PHILOSOPHY
578 BC
–1847 AD

Marx and others have announced the death of philosphy. (This makes things difficult for professional philosophers.) An Italian called **Gramsci** said *everyone* was a philosopher of sorts.

A lot earlier **Plato** had said things would only be all right when philosophers ruled the world. Other philosophers have argued that philosophy teaches that there is no meaning to anything at all, which could make ruling difficult.

CONFUSED?

Let us leave it to **Bertie Russell** to give us a definition to be going on with:

PHILOSOPHY IS THE NO-MAN'S LAND BETWEEN *SCIENCE* AND *THEOLOGY*, EXPOSED TO ATTACK FROM BOTH SIDES

Oddly enough there seems to be general agreement on **when** philosophy started....

WHY **THEN?** Well, listen to the German philosopher **Karl Jaspers**:

THE AXIS OF WORLD HISTORY SEEMS TO PASS THROUGH THE FIFTH CENTURY BC IN THE MIDST OF THE SPIRITUAL PROCESS BETWEEN 800 AND 200 BC WHICH SAW **CONFUCIUS**, **LAO-TSE** IN CHINA, THE **UPANISHADS** AND **BUDDHA** IN INDIA, **ZARATHUSTRA** IN PERSIA, THE OLD TESTAMENT **PROPHETS** IN PALESTINE, **HOMER**, THE **PHILOSOPHERS** AND **TRAGEDIANS** IN GREECE

The Pre-Socratics
Bhagavad-Gita
Mahayana Buddhism
The Diamond Sutra
Aeschylus
Sophocles
Isaiah
Tao-te-Ching
Analects
The Odyssey

Clearly, there were intellectual stirrings on a wide-scale

.. and there's general agreement on **where** it started ...

G R E E C E

WHY **GREECE?**

By the 6th century BC the city-states on mainland Greece were thriving commercial centres. The Greeks were developing, through their dramatic arts, the idea of the rule of necessity, rather than blind chance. They were building the basic structure of democracy. They had inherited the adventurous sea-faring spirit of the earlier Minoan civilisation. They travelled widely. They had a language suited to precise description. They had assimilated geometry from the Egyptians, and star-lore and knowledge of the calendar from Asia Minor. This early history is not at all certain, however.

FOR WANT OF SOMEONE BETTER TO BLAME FOR STARTING PHILOSOPHY WE'LL PICK **THALES**

Thales

was the first man to whom the name of "wise" was given. He was a politician, geometer, astronomer and thinker in the busy port of Miletus. He is credited with correctly predicting the solar eclipse in 585 BC. He wasn't interested in myth but in knowledge of the world and the stars. He was a practical thinker.

WHAT WAS UNIQUE ABOUT GREEKS LIKE THALES WAS THAT THEY TRIED TO DISENTANGLE SCIENCE AND MAGIC, AND DARED TO THINK ABOUT THE WORLD WITHOUT FIRST THINKING OF GOD

PERHAPS, IN THE BEGINNING, EVERYTHING WAS MADE OF **WATER**..

Thales' question isn't as wet as it sounds — but more importantly, it's a **NEW** kind of question

What these early philosophers were looking for was the **unity of things**.

Anaximander,

alive around 546 BC was in the same tradition.
He held that the earth was freely suspended in space.
He suggested that all living creatures arose from water, and that men had evolved from fish.
He argued that there was a single primal substance and a natural law which exerts itself in the world, maintaining a balance between different elements.

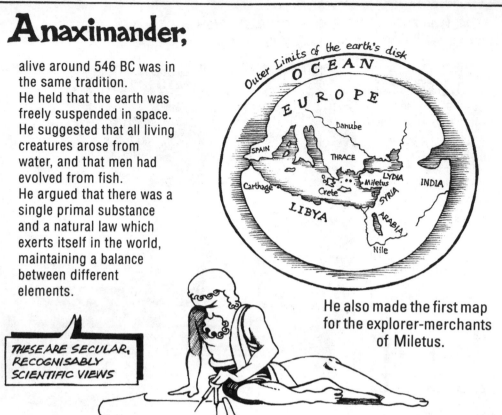

He also made the first map for the explorer-merchants of Miletus.

THESE ARE SECULAR, RECOGNISABLY SCIENTIFIC VIEWS

Pythagoras
was a curious blend of scientist and mystic

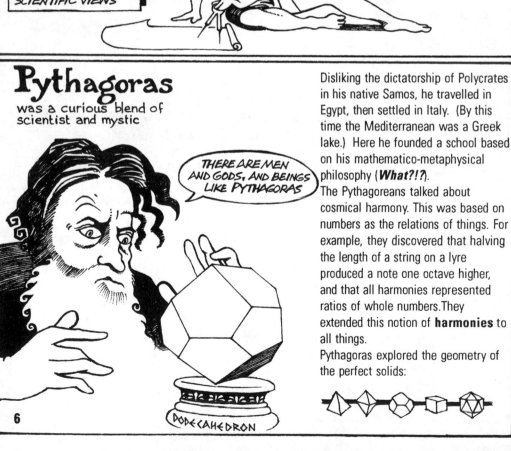

THERE ARE MEN AND GODS, AND BEINGS LIKE PYTHAGORAS

DODECAHEDRON

Disliking the dictatorship of Polycrates in his native Samos, he travelled in Egypt, then settled in Italy. (By this time the Mediterranean was a Greek lake.) Here he founded a school based on his mathematico-metaphysical philosophy (**What?!?**).

The Pythagoreans talked about cosmical harmony. This was based on numbers as the relations of things. For example, they discovered that halving the length of a string on a lyre produced a note one octave higher, and that all harmonies represented ratios of whole numbers. They extended this notion of **harmonies** to all things.

Pythagoras explored the geometry of the perfect solids:

6

He discovered the theorem that still bears his name.

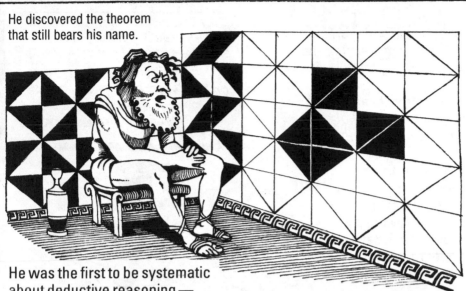

He was the first to be systematic about deductive reasoning — starting with an axiom that is self-evident, then proceeding step by logical step to a conclusion that is far from self-evident.

THIS GAVE A GREAT IMPETUS TO SCIENCE, BUT THE SEARCH FOR THE **SELF-EVIDENT** HAS TORMENTED PHILOSOPHERS THROUGH THE AGES

NOT CONTENT WITH SHOWING THE IMPORTANT PART PLAYED BY NUMBERS IN THE UNIVERSE, **PYTHAGORAS** SAID:

THE SOUL IS AN IMMORTAL THING, AND IS TRANSFORMED INTO OTHER LIVING THINGS—WHATEVER COMES INTO EXISTENCE IS BORN AGAIN IN THE REVOLUTIONS OF A CERTAIN CYCLE—NOTHING BEING ABSOLUTELY NEW

Pythagoras' advances in mathematics led him to overvalue the power of numbers.
He believed the dodecahedron somehow embodied the structure of the entire Universe.
He elevated his discoveries in music into a cosmic theory of the harmony of the spheres.

ALL THINGS ARE NUMBERS

PYTHAGORAS WASN'T THE **LAST** PHILOSOPHER TO BE BEGUILED BY THE BEAUTY AND CERTAINTY OF MATHEMATICS

7

He also formed a Pythagorean Order, with a set of complex and seemingly arbitrary taboos which included:

> To abstain from beans
> Not to eat a from a whole loaf
> Not to sit on a quart measure

A REMINDER OF HOW CLOSE THE ANCIENT GREEKS WERE TO THE WORLD OF **SUPERSTITION** & THE **IRRATIONAL**? OR, MORE SINISTERLY, AN INSTANCE OF THE IMPULSE OF PHILOSOPHERS TO SAFEGUARD KNOWLEDGE UNDER THE DOMAIN OF A PRIESTLY CASTE?

A member of the Order, **Hippasos**, was banished, not for eating, but for spilling the beans about the Order's most closely guarded secret — that the

THIS IS AB-SURD..

of this triangle was a surd — it could not be written as a ratio of whole numbers.

Heraclitus

alive around 500 BC, argued that everything was in a state of flux. But he believed, too, in a cosmic justice that maintained equilibrium in the world. This was a complex idea! His choice for the one primary element everyone was seeking: **FIRE**. There was a central fire that never dies...

YOU CANNOT STEP INTO THE SAME RIVER TWICE

AGAIN PREFIGURING MODERN SCIENTIFIC IDEAS

The Glory that was Greece

There was an extraordinary flowering of culture in classical Greece.
Passionate and enquiring, the Greeks produced ideas and artefacts out of all proportion to the general development of the society of the time.

There were statesmen like **Pericles**, tragedians like **Euripides**, sculptors like **Phidias**, historians, musicians, potters, painters, lyric poets like **Sappho**, satirists like **Aristophanes**, architects, mathematicians as well as philosophers.

BUT IT MUST BE REMEMBERED THAT THE NEWLY-INVENTED DEMOCRACIES WERE BASED ON SLAVERY — ONLY ONE-SIXTH OF THE MEMBERS OF A CITY-STATE WERE CITIZENS, ONCE YOU COUNTED OUT SLAVES, CHILDREN, FOREIGNERS (BARBARIANS THE GREEKS CALLED THEM) AND WOMEN (WHO HAD ALMOST NO CIVIL RIGHTS).
THIS WAS TO DEFORM THEIR ATTEMPTS TO DEVELOP ETHICAL AND POLITICAL PHILOSOPHIES.

Empedocles

NEXT THE STRANGE EMPEDOCLES OF AGRAGAS
EXPERIMENTING WITH A WATER-CLOCK OF BRASS

HE WROTE IN VERSE, DISCOVERED AIR
HE THOUGHT HE WAS GOD — SO THERE

HE ARGUED THAT THERE WERE FOUR ELEMENTS IN ALL
THAT PLANTS HAD SEX, THE EARTH WAS LIKE A BALL

THAT CHANGE TOOK PLACE BY LOVE AND STRIFE
AND HISTORIC CYCLES RAN THROUGH LIFE

WHEN CALLED UPON TO PROVE HIS DEITY
HE SNEERED AT ALL THE WAITING LAITY

GREAT EMPEDOCLES, THAT ARDENT SOUL
LEAPT INTO ETNA, AND WAS ROASTED WHOLE

The Atomists
(c 420 BC)

Leucippus & Democritus

took from their predecessor Parmenides
the idea of basic elementary particles,
and from Heraclitus, endless movement.
They proposed innumerable tiny solid
particles — atoms — which could not be
cut.
The atoms flew around randomly, and
were too small to be seen.
The ever-changing world was explained
as a ceaseless rearrangemnt of the
unchanging atoms into different shapes.
Not until the chemist Dalton in 1800 AD
was there a significant advance on this
theory.

DEMOCRITUS SAID THE REASON YOU COULD CUT AN
APPLE WITH A KNIFE WAS BECAUSE THERE WERE
SPACES BETWEEN THE ATOMS. HIS THEORY WAS
A FUSION OF SUCH PRACTICAL THINKING AND
THE TRADITION OF ABSTRACT THOUGHT ON FUNDAMENTALS

10

Big change: THE SOPHISTS

Where earlier Greek philosophers had been interested in the universe, in unity and difference, in the big questions, the **SOPHISTS** were more interested in Man himself, how he behaved. Instead of looking for a big truth, the Sophists were more interested in the mechanics of how man could do things for himself. This led them into teaching people how to write, to make speeches, and how to win court cases through the use of paradox and twisted argument. This got them into trouble in Athens for leading people into bad habits (like being cynical).

Protagoras

MAN IS THE MEASURE OF ALL THINGS

AN ESSENTIALLY PRACTICAL MAN, PROTAGORAS THOUGHT REAL KNOWLEDGE WASN'T POSSIBLE. WHAT MATTERED WAS **USEFUL OPINION** THIS IS A DEEP SCEPTICISM WHERE DISAGREEMENTS CANNOT BE DECIDED BY AN APPEAL TO THE TRUTH

THIS UTTER RELATIVISM LED TO THRASYMACHUS' CRUDE **MIGHT IS RIGHT** CONCLUSIONS

JUSTICE IS THE ADVANTAGE OF THE STRONGER

Thrasymachus

Socrates
(470-399 BC)

THE UNEXAMINED LIFE IS NOT WORTH LIVING

Initially people thought Socrates was a sophist, but in fact he was their bitterest opponent.

He wrote nothing himself, but from the general **Xenophon** and philosopher **Plato** we get a very real picture of the man.

Shabbily dressed, always barefoot, physically tough, and with a record of courage in battle, he loved to spend his days arguing in the market-place.

With Socrates there is a shift away from the scientific querying we have seen so far to the problem of Ethics.. He was deeply concerned with morality, with discovering the just, the true, and the good.

For Socrates philosophy wasn't a profession, as with the sophists, but a way of life.

11

When the Oracle at Delphi said 'None is wiser than Socrates', he chose to interpret it thus: He is wisest amongst men who sees, like Socrates, that his wisdom is paltry.

Socrates argued that what makes a man sin is lack of knoweldge. If only he knew he would not sin. Knowledge was Virtue. The one overriding cause of Evil was Ignorance. This is a very un-Christian ethical stance.

He preferred to see himself as a GAD-FLY, stirring up the lazy.

The Dialectic

Socrates' method of enquiry was one of question and answer. He saw himself as midwife to the truth, which he would draw logically, and often ironically, little by little from his opponent.
James Joyce suggested that he learnt this useful discovery from his wife Xanthippe.

The aim of Socrates' s dialectic and irony was to expose false claims to wisdom and to move towards a knowledge of man's own nature. Socrates was not cynical about the possibility of truth but was convinced it could only be achieved through hard work.

Plato (428–354 BC)

ΑCADEMY

ΜΗΔΕΙΣ ΑΓΕΩΜΕΤΡΗΤΟΣ ΕΙΣΙΤΩ

"LET NO-ONE IGNORANT OF GEOMETRY ENTER HERE"

CHEAP RATE WISDOM

THIS'LL PUT US OUT OF BUSINESS

IT WON'T LAST*

* IT LASTED 900 YEARS!

This was the prototype of all universitites. The basic studies were arithmetic, geometry, astronomy and the harmonics of sound. The Academy had scientific equipment and a library. The aim was to train men's minds to enable them to think for themselves in the light of reason.

The method seems to have been research under supervision. Education required a joint effort on the part of teacher and pupil — a truly dialectical process. Star pupil and school swot was **Aristotle** — who studied at the Academy for 20 years.

THE THEORY of IDEAS

Plato said the general word 'horse' refers not to this horse but to any horse. There is, somewhere or other, an ideal horse, outside space and time. The idea is real, the particular is only apparent.

THIS APPARENTLY INNOCENT OBSERVATION WAS TO BE THE CAUSE OF MORE LOST MARBLES AMONG PHILOSOPHERS THAN WERE EVER NICKED FROM THE PARTHENON.

To illustrate the difference between appearance and reality, Plato came up with his famous SIMILE of the CAVE.

NOT **THIS**

OR **THAT**

BUT SOMEHOW **THIS**

EVERYONE IS CHAINED IN A CAVE. THE PRISONERS SEE ONLY SHADOWS AND TAKE THEM FOR REALITY

ONE MAN ESCAPES. HE LEAVES THE CAVE AND SEES THE REAL WORLD

BUT...

AH SHADDUP!

HE RETURNS, BUT DAZZLED BY THE LIGHT, SEEMS MORE STUPID THAN BEFORE.

13

REASON
&
TRUTH

Plato was a prolific writer, not of text-books, but of elegant and lively dialogues in the style of thrillers with truth as the quarry.

Socrates is often the main character —so there is a problem of what is Socrates and what is Plato. But it seems clear that in the later dialogues Plato is developing his own ideas.

It is THE PHILOSOPHER who sees things in the sunlight, which represents the GOOD.

ANAMNESIS

In Plato's theory of education there is a notion that knowledge is remembering or anamnesis. The soul or mind has passed through a previous series of embodied and disembodied states, and the knowledge from these previous cycles needs merely to be awakened. Socrates appears, in the midwife role, eliciting from an untutored lad the construction of a square twice the area of a given square.

The THIRD MAN problem

Particular Man

IDEA of MAN

Between a particular man and Plato's form or idea of a man, you can place a **third man** who is somehow less particular. For instance he has no warts. But then you can place another between **him** and the idea, and so on ad infinitum....

14

For Plato the **BIG QUESTION** was
'WHAT IS KNOWLEDGE?'

Is it sense perception?
No — to rely on the mere senses, on appearances, is no better than Protagoras.

Is it purely mental?
No — for then it would be impossible to commit an error.

So it is an interaction between perceiver and perceived, under the guidance of an overall sense, the soul or mind. It is the soul which apprehends things like identity, difference, existence and number.

Plato improved the theory of hypothesis (literally a putting-underneath) and deduction.

He showed how a hypothesis had to explain the facts or 'save the appearances'. If a fact didn't square with a hypothesis then a new hypothesis was needed.

And the search was always for a bigger, better, more general hypothesis. The ultimate search was for the giant **H** which explains the good.

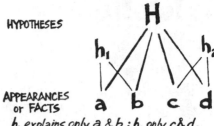

HYPOTHESES

APPEARANCES or FACTS

h_1 explains only a & b ; h_2 only c & d.
H explains all four, and so destroys the special hypotheses h_1 & h_2.

Plato's Politics

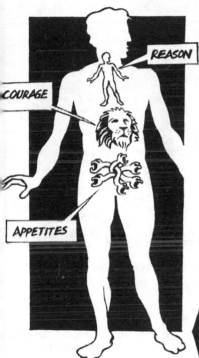

REASON

COURAGE

APPETITES

In the Republic, Plato outlines his ideal city-state. This is the grand-daddy of all Utopias. He was much influenced by the model of the severe Spartan society.

He takes 3 classes:

| The elite guardians |
| The soldiers |
| The masses (HOI POLLOI) |

He takes 3 structures:

| Monarchy |
| Oligarchy (rule by a few) |
| Democracy |

He provides for some social mobility, but doesn't challenge slavery. Much emphasis is put upon training the élite. In an unideal world Plato plumps for the rule of the ONE and the MANY, a mixed constitution of monarchy and democracy.

The individual soul is divided into three. This structure repeats itself in the state:

REASON	COURAGE	APPETITES
Elite guardians	Soldiers	Masses

PLATO WAS THE FATHER OF IDEALISM AND THE UNCLE OF RELIGION, AS WELL AS THE GRANDFATHER OF ALMOST ALL SYSTEMS OF RIGOROUS THEORETICAL SPECULATION. BECAUSE HE SOUGHT PERFECTION HE MOVED AWAY FROM THE MESSY WORLD OF PARTICULARS AND TOWARDS THE ABSTRACT, IDEAL WORLD OF THOUGHT. IN BEING IDEALIST HE WAS, HOWEVER, RIGOROUS AND THIS CONTRADICTION RUNS THROUGH HIS WORK.

Aristotle

Aristotle was the last, and the most influential of the great Greek philosophers.
Born in 384 BC at Stagyra in Thrace, he was sent by his father, a court physican, to Plato's Academy.

PLATO IS DEAR TO ME, BUT DEARER STILL IS TRUTH

WE MUST NOT FEEL A CHILDISH DISGUST AT THE INVESTIGATION OF THE MEANER ANIMALS. FOR THERE IS SOMETHING MARVELLOUS IN ALL NATURAL THINGS

He only got a grade C in mathematics, but A for effort otherwise, and starred in natural history.
Then he travelled widely, and began developing and making systematic his own ideas.
He challenged Plato's idealism most directly in his empirical approach to the study of nature.
In Lesbos he did original work in marine biology.

For three years he was tutor to Alexander

DON'T WORRY ABOUT IT — I'M OFF TO CONQUER THE KNOWN WORLD NEXT WEEK

ALEXANDER THE GREAT WAS TO FIGHT BATTLES FROM THE NILE IN THE WEST TO THE INDUS IN THE EAST, HELLENISING EGYPTIANS, PERSIANS AND SEMITES ON THE WAY. HIS ATTEMPT AT EMPIRE MARKED THE END OF THE CLASSICAL PERIOD, OF WHICH ARISTOTLE WAS A CHILD.

In 335 he founded his own school in Athens, the Lyceum. As a centre of systematic research it far outstripped the Academy.
When teaching, Aristotle would walk and talk, and from this habit, the Lyceum students became known as the peripatetics.

In 323 Alexander died. Athens rose against Macedonia, and because of his years as tutor, a charge of impiety was brought against Aristotle. No lover of hemlock, he quietly left Athens, and died two years later.

TO SAVE THE ATHENIANS FROM SINNING TWICE AGAINST PHILOSOPHY

ARISTOTLE WAS VIRTUALLY CANONISED BY THE MEDIEVAL SCHOOLMEN AS A PAGAN SAINT. MANY OF HIS IDEAS, ODDLY WELDED TO CHRISTIAN OR ISLAMIC FAITH, WERE CARRIED DOWN THROUGH THE AGES AS DOGMA AND REMAINED UNCHALLENGED FOR ALMOST

2,000 YEARS

Of course he can't be blamed for the way posterity made him an infallible authority.

Aristotle left many writings — most of them closely-argued treatises. He is not an entertaining writer like Plato, and from being revered by the Church scholars, became reviled in the Renaissance, and the stigma of the boring professor has stuck to him.

But in scope, and often in precision, he surpasses Plato.

He was the first to divide and subdivide the areas of enquiry — the first to attempt a classification of knowledge.

Andronicus of Rhodes put the treatises into order about 50 BC. He placed a series of writings after the **PHYSICS** & called them **META-PHYSICS** (literally AFTER-PHYSICS)

Logic

Aristotle said the basic building-block of all argument was the
SYLLOGISM

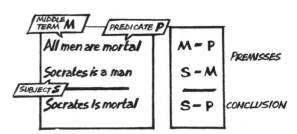

MIDDLE TERM **M** — PREDICATE **P**	
All men are mortal	M — P
Socrates is a man	S — M
SUBJECT **S**	
Socrates is mortal	S — P

PREMISSES

CONCLUSION

Aristotle then listed all possible syllogisms, and showed which were valid and which were not.

Logic was a tool to be sharpened in the pursuit of knowledge

MATHEMATICIANS LIKE **EULER**, AND LATER, **BOOLE** AND **LEWIS CARROL** DEVELOPED THE STUDY OF LOGIC CONSIDERABLY – AND MODERN PHILOSOPHERS LIKE **RUSSELL** AND **WHITEHEAD** DEVELOPED A WHOLE LANGUAGE OF ARGUMENT BASED ON LOGICAL CONSISTENCY.

The Categories

Aristotle's work on logic led him to study the structure of language. He distinguished between the knowledge of the meanings of words, and the knowledge of judgements made with those words. He came up with ten different general items in speech — the CATEGORIES. These were what words meant on their own.

SVBSTANCE
QVALITY
QVANTITY
RELATION
PLACE
TIME
POSITION
STATE
ACTION
AFFECTION

BONE
EDIBLE
SIX INCHES
MINE
WHERE DID I BVRY IT?
YESTERDAY
IN THE GROVND
SVCCVLENT
LYING STILL
BEING SOVGHT

LINGUISTICS STARTS HERE. AND ALSO THE BYZANTINE. COMPLEXITIES OF MODERN LINGUISTIC PHILOSOPHY

Metaphysics

Aristotle's efforts here went towards producing a rival theory to Plato's forms. He was opposed, like Plato, to the sophistic relativism of the likes of Protagoras, but he felt that the Forms caused neither movement nor change, nor helped to understand what is real and what is knowable.
Instead he proposed that Substance was a fusion of Matter and Form.

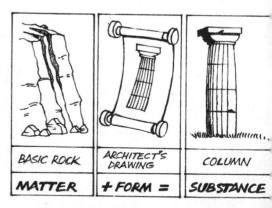

BASIC ROCK	ARCHITECT'S DRAWING	COLUMN
MATTER	+ FORM =	SUBSTANCE

To explain change, Aristotle used the ideas of actuality and potentiality.
The substance is the potential bearer of qualities that become actual in it.
Thus, to say oil is inflammable is to say that the potential for it to burn is present in it, but it needs an applied match to bring out the potential to burn.

Aristotle shows his biological bent here, where dynamic Becoming is more important than Plato's timeless Being.

But Aristotle went further in his theory of Causality.
He said there were four causes of the stone falling:

MATERIAL	1 The stone itself
FORMAL	2 The lie of the land
EFFICIENT	3 The push
FINAL	4 The stone's desire to seek the lowest level

Aristotle said 'Nature does not act without a goal.' This works well in biology or ethics, but is a great hindrance in physics.

In modern causality only the efficient cause would be considered. The final cause brings in the notion of a goal, and interpretation in terms of final purpose or **teleology**.

And the final final cause behind everything, a philosopher's Nobodaddy God — the UNMOVED MOVER.

DOCTRINE OF FINAL CLAUSE

THE DOCTRINE ITSELF DIDN'T FALL UNTIL GALILEO

Ethics

Aristotle had a more monistic view of the soul than Plato.

IF THE EYE WERE A LIVING CREATURE, SIGHT WOULD BE ITS SOUL

But he singled out one faculty — *active reason* — as somehow separate from the body, and immortal.

He rejected Plato's absolutism about ethics:

IT IS AS INAPPROPRIATE TO DEMAND DEMONSTRATION IN ETHICS AS IT IS TO ALLOW A MATHEMATICIAN TO USE MERELY PROBABLE ARGUMENTS

19

Good was explained as 'that at which all things aim' — the active reason's search for virtue.
Virtue involves choice, and the correct choice was the **Mean**.

Thus courage is neither rash aggressiveness

SEE YOU JIMMY

.. nor timid withdrawal

BUT HOW WOULD YOU DEFINE THE VIRTUE OF **HONESTY** IN THIS WAY?

Politics

Artistotle didn't go beyond Plato's city-state model. At a time when empire was in the offing, he talked about the perfect workings of a city no bigger than could be taken in at a glance from a hill-top.
One research project at the Lyceum collected and compared 158 different city-state constitutions.

MAN IS A POLITICAL ANIMAL

MENIAL AND MECHANICAL OCCUPATIONS UNFIT A MAN FOR CITIZENSHIP

ETHICAL ELITE VILLAS

His formula for political stability was a strong middle class, to create a MEAN between tyranny and democracy.
Aristotle didn't challenge slavery and though women were unfit for freedom and political rights.
But he did provide in his will for the freeing of his slaves.
His notion of the enlightened gentleman has persisted, especially through the English public school system.

Biology

In his detailed studies, Aristotle refers to over 500 different species.
He insisted on the study of particulars – 'what is better known to us' – before theorising. He took on the enormous task of the classification of life forms.

His work here mirrors his more general attempt at the classification of knowledge.

Poetics

Aristotle thought poetry was more serious than history, because it dealt in universals. His theory of the aim of tragedy — through pity and fear — to achieve a purging or catharsis of these emotions, has persisted to this day.

BARF!

Aristotle muses on Catharsis

20

Alexandria

Founded by Alexander in 332 BC on a natural harbour at one of the mouths of the Nile, it soon flourished under the enlightened rule of the Macedonian **Ptolemy I** into the greatest Mediterranean sea-port. The city was intensely cosmopolitan, bringing together Egyptians, the Jews of the Diaspora, and other races besides Greeks.

For 600 years, while Alexander's ephemeral Hellenic empire split and faltered, and imperial Rome rose and fell, Alexandria was the last great light of antiquity.

In the Museum dazzling advances in science were made, and the Library, with its huge staff of copyists, became an unrivalled centre of learning.

SCIENCE LIBERATES US FROM THE TERROR OF THE GODS

Galen DEVELOPED THE MEDICAL WORK OF HIPPOCRATES & PRODUCED THE FIRST ANATOMY

Diophantus MADE THE FIRST BEGINNINGS IN ALGEBRA

THERE IS NO ROYAL ROAD TO MATHEMATICS

Ctesibius INVENTED AN ADVANCED WATER-CLOCK

Euclid RIGOROUSLY SYSTEMATISED GEOMETRY & STUDIED LIGHT REFLECTION

Apollonius BEGAN THE STUDY OF CURVES WITH SECTIONS OF CONES

GIVE ME SOMEWHERE TO STAND AND I WILL MOVE THE EARTH

Hipparchus TABULATED 1080 FIXED STARS, COMPILED THE FIRST TRIGONOMETRICAL TABLES

Aristarchus CALCULATED THE MOON'S DIAMETER WITH ONLY 8% ERROR PROPOSED THAT THE EARTH MOVED ROUND THE SUN (Eat your heart out Copernicus)

Archimedes DEVELOPED THE PHYSICS OF LEVERS, BUOYANCY & HYDRAULICS, & INVENTED COMPLEX WAR-MACHINES

21

Forms of Scepticism

Meanwhile, back at the Academy and the Lyceum, things weren't going so well . . .

The confident questioning outlook of the citizen-aristocrat like Plato has gone.

With **Antisthenes** a new scepticism arises, which was to be absorbed into the Academy in its years of decline. He argued that it was impossible to make significant statements.

> WHAT I AM NOW SAYING IS A LIE

Epimenides

> IF THIS IS TRUE. IT'S FALSE, & IF IT'S FALSE IT'S TRUE! **True or false?**

Clever paradox-mongering like this became fashionable.

Pyrrho even got systematic about it, and made doubt itself central.

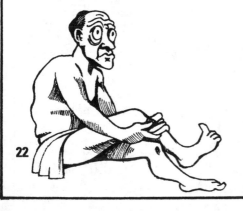

A colourful disciple of Antisthenes was **Diogenes** (c.350BC).

He lived a life as primitive as a dog. From the Greek *kuvikos* = dog-like, we get the word cynicism.

Legend has it he lived in a tub, and to show contempt for public opinion, masturbated in the market place. . .

EARLY CYNIC ROLE MODEL

> And now, in the absence of much philosophy to talk about, we take a short break into history. . .
> But as Hegel said:
>
> PHILOSOPHY IS THE STUDY OF ITS OWN HISTORY

The Grandeur that was Rome...

Rome grew out of the bitter and prolonged Punic wars with Carthage — as a city-state it evolved as a war-machine.

The Romans added almost nothing new to philosophy. Where the Greeks *thought* a lot, the Romans *fought* a lot.

So we talk of Greek CIVILISATION, but of the Roman EMPIRE. Rome's supreme role was to transmit a culture older and superior to its own.

EASY!

I FORGOT MY SANDWICHES

HAVE THE CHRISTIANS BEEN ON YET?

THESE MATINEE AUDIENCES ARE KILLERS

The Roman Empire lasted about four centuries in all.

GAUL

SPAIN

DALMATIA

GALATIA

NUMIDIA

EGYPT

SPQR

The ROMAN EMPIRE at the death of AUGUSTUS AD 14

Great advances in practical thought were made-cement, the arch, sewerage systems and the civil service, but the philosophy was all Greek inspired.

'THE FORM IN WHICH GREECE MIGRATED TO ROME' as Marx said, was **Stoicism**.

Chrysippus (d 207 BC)

is credited with the first systematic account of Stoicism, and an interest in logic and language.

WHY DON'T GET A QUOTE?

ANSWER: Because in 47 BC Julius Caesar's legions burn the library at Alexandria

---

The founder of Stoicism proper was the Greek

Zeno (d 261 BC)

Zeno ran his own school in Athens where the Stoics lived the simple life they argued for philosophically. His teachings started from logic, passed to physics and then to ethics. Stoicism's main impact over the centuries was in the ethical field. To be stoical was to face destiny with courage and dignity.

For a Stoic the highest good was a life of virtue. Prudence, justice, temperance, and courage were the routes to virtue. The Stoics saw the world as an organic whole in which the laws of nature were determinant.

A materialist who followed many of Democritus's ideas was

Epicurus (d 270 BC)

A CHEERFUL POVERTY IS AN HONOURABLE STATE

Although his philosophy appears similar to Stoicism it is different in its consistency and its refusal of the idea of fate. The prime good was pleasure, which was seen as the avoidance of suffering. Epicureanism was not, as it has come to mean, an idea of wallowing in pleasure, but a philosophy that attempted to achieve equilibrium.

Epicurus advocated the achievement of inner peace. Banishing fear and religion were important, particularly the fear of death.

WE NEED TO SET OUR AFFECTIONS ON SOME GOOD MAN & KEEP HIM CONSTANTLY BEFORE OUR EYES, SO THAT WE MAY LIVE AS IF HE WERE WATCHING US, AND DO EVERYTHING AS IF HE SAW WHAT WE WERE DOING

For Epicurus the good man is, of course, Socrates

For Epicurus the importance of philosophy was to free men from ignorance and superstition.

Lucretius (99-55 BC)
helped to absorb stoicism into the Roman world

In his great poem *De Rerum Natura*, he sets out Epicurus' doctrine. It includes the first clear

statement of the law of conservation of matter:
'Nothing can be created out of nothing.'

Seneca
(4 BC – 65 AD)

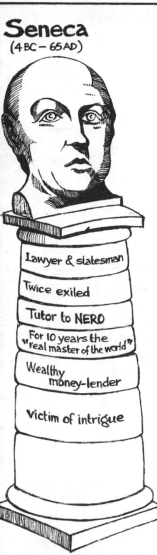

Lawyer & statesman

Twice exiled

Tutor to NERO

"For 10 years the 'real master of the world'"

Wealthy money-lender

Victim of intrigue

In a series of stylish letters aimed at posterity, he outlines the virtuous Stoic's ideals.

Philosophy appears as good advice. . .

Seneca is vividly aware of the divided will — there's a strong sense that being good is hard work. For Plato and Aristotle the problem of the will doesn't really arise.

In Aristotle's Ethics, it's clear that the ease and pleasure with which good acts are done, the absence of moral effort, is for him the symptom of virtue.

*However, he **did** challenge slavery, and preferred death to accommodating Nero's endless whims*

WE ROMANS ARE EXCEPTIONALLY ARROGANT, HARSH & INSULTING TO OUR SLAVES ... YOU SHOULD TREAT YOUR INFERIORS IN THE WAY IN WHICH YOU WOULD LIKE TO BE TREATED BY YOUR OWN SUPERIORS

TACITUS GIVES A GRIM ACCOUNT OF THE SUICIDE – CUT WRISTS, KNEES & ANKLES AND POISON...

But Seneca is a great hypocrite too: deploring yet courting fame, arguing poverty as a millionaire, writing fawning letters from exile. The philosopher dying for his beliefs — Socrates accepting the fatal hemlock — appears first as a tragedy. With Seneca history repeats itself as farce.

Epictetus
(60 AD – 100 AD)

THE LIFE OF EVERY MAN IS A SOLDIER'S SERVICE. AND THAT LONG AND VARIOUS

The Greek Epictetus was born a slave, but gained his freedom. This may have affected his philosophy.

Epictetus didn't agree with the formal division of philosophy into logic, physics and ethics and brought to a logical conclusion Stoicism's tendency to reduce philosophy to ethics. What Epictetus did was to bring out the whole problem of free will and determinism that was implicit in Stoicism.

25

Marcus Aurelius

(120–180 AD)

Marcus Aurelius' rule as emperor marks the end of the Pax Romana.
The Empire, rimmed by barbarian hordes, was in decline. There had been no growth in its bounds for half a century, and no growth in its political thinking.

The Decline and Fall of the Roman Empire
...∞...
Edward Gibbon
1737–1794

'All that is human must retrograde if it does not advance'

From his writings in Greek, usually called the Meditations, we get a vivid picture of a fastidious, care-worn insomniac endlessly rehearsing death.

THE HUNS ARE COMING!

DEATH REDUCED TO THE SAME CONDITION ALEXANDER & HIS MULETEER

EXECUTE EVERY ACT OF YOUR LIFE AS THOUGH IT WERE YOUR LAST

AS ONE ALREADY DYING, DISDAIN THE FLESH

'ALL THE THINGS OF THE BODY ARE AS A RIVER AND THE THINGS OF THE SOUL A DREAM; LIFE IS A WAR AND FAME AFTER DEATH FORGETFULNESS'.

He bullies himself to be sincere, dignified, hard-working, kindly, independent, frugal, serious & high-minded...
To disdain fame...

THE PURPLE-EDGED ROBE IS ONLY SHEEP'S WOOL STEEPED IN THE BLOOD OF A SHELL-FISH

SEXUAL INTERCOURSE IS ONLY AN INTERNAL RUBBING & SPASMODIC EXCRETION OF MUCUS

To abstain from pleasure...

SOCIAL OBLIGATION IS THE LEADING FEATURE IN THE CONSTITUTION OF MAN— THAT WHICH IS NOT IN THE INTEREST OF THE HIVE CANNOT BE IN THE INTEREST OF THE BEE

HEAVY METAL

The great Greco-Roman period was coming to an end. It had been the most extraordinary flourishing of free-thinking ever known. Everything had come under consideration from one point of view or another. This was the **GREAT LEAP FORWARD**.

People had refused to accept simple explanations for things and were willing to pursue an argument to its conclusion. There might be different conclusions, but the whole point was the <u>method</u> of thinking that the Greeks developed.

The Pre-Socratic philosophers all tended to look for **universal principles** to explain the whole of Nature. This was a step forward from just accepting myth. **Socrates** turned the spotlight on Man himself, trying to work out how to live properly, to tell the difference between right and wrong, good and evil. Socrates had said *"The unexamined life is not worth living."* His dialectical method of trying to ferret out the truth is probably as close as anyone got to being the basis of philosophy.

All of these early philosophers were looking for the **TRUTH** and had to try and find a method of working out what it was. **Plato** and **Aristotle** between them organized and systematized most of the problems that were to become known as philosophy, quite a hard act to follow. The early Greeks had started from the question of Man's nature, and his place in the universe, and constructed a whole method of reasoning out of that questioning. **Plato** and **Aristotle** gave these modes of thinking a conceptual clarity and rigour which laid the foundations for all philosophy.

We haven't answered the question of why it was the Greeks who started all of this, but we know what the questions were.

The question *"How do I know?"* kept popping up behind all of the different approaches. Combined with the question *"What is the world made of?"* this mode of thinking made life difficult for the average Greek. This is how philosophy got its reputation as being difficult and awkward. History was to make life even more awkward over the next few centuries.

One event that went unrecorded in philosophy at the time but which had rather severe after-effects was the **rise of Christianity.** An obscure carpenter, a virgin, and a donkey were the original ingredients. Christianity is supposedly about the Bible and Christ, but that's just what they tell the punters.

It started off from myth, Moses, parables, stories about Jesus, and bits of mystical philosophy from here and there. Unlike philosophy, religion had an answer for everything — and the answer was usually **God**. Christianity had lots of rivals other than Judaism. There was the cult of Isis, Mithraism, the official divinities, and Orphic Mysticism. In fact, Christianity could have died out like lots of other cult shows. But instead it ran and ran...

Jesus Christ SuperStar

It was **St. Paul** who saved Christianity from dying out or settling down as just another Jewish sect. He combined it with Greek philosophy and came up with a winning formula. Christianity and philosophy were to have an intimate and developing relationship for well over 1,000 years.

Philo *of Alexandria*
(25 BC – 50 AD)

Christ and NeoPlatonism

Various people added bits to Christianity.

Philo was a contemporary of Christ and an orthodox Jew, who was into showing how philosophy prepared the mind for higher things (God). He was basically a Platonist who turned the abstract Universals of Plato back into God. This was to set a precedent.

Philosophy got steadily more metaphysical and more concerned with the structure of the soul than with science or politics, or even ethics. It may have been something to do with the Roman Empire falling apart that led to more interest in religion, but combining Greek rationalism with Judeo-Christian thought became all the rage. Pure philosophy got more and more watered down.

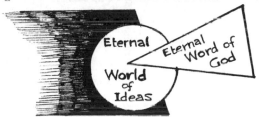

Origen (184 – 254 AD)

thought that the

Christians might use philosophy by borrowing the best ideas from it.
He saw that Plato's notion of the sensible world as a mere reflection of the higher intelligible world seemed to accord with Christianity.
Like the other Christian Platonists he expounded the Bible as a symbolist allegory.
What was impossible for him was that the text should have only a literal meaning.

AND THERE BE EUNUCHS WHICH HAVE MADE THEMSELVES EUNUCHS FOR THE KINGDOM OF HEAVEN'S SAKE

Origen's opposition to literalism is odd in light of the story that he took Matthew XIX 12 literally himself...

Plotinus

(204 – 270 AD) was a curious late Platonist

The most other-worldly of philosophers, Plotinus ignored Plato's social and political thought and made philosophy itself a religion.

The most important part of his thought was the conception of a **HOLY TRINITY** that structured the world

This was based on Plato's notion of the **Ideas**

For Plotinus there was:

The ONE

The God — an abstract godliness emanating power as the Sun emanates light

The NOUS or SPIRIT

Looks up to the ONE, of which it is an image, & down to all other things

The SOUL

The human soul which looks up to contemplate the NOUS & through it the idea of God

The soul looks down to the body

THE SUPREME ACHIEVEMENT OF THE INTELLECT IS TO LEAVE ITSELF BEHIND

Below the soul is matter & nature and are thus the most formless, shapeless & imperfect things   They are farthest from the ONE

Neo-Platonism

This term was invented later on to describe the attempt to produce an all-embracing synthesis of philosophy and religious ideals. From Plotinus there was a complex system at the heart of which was this idea of the 'One', a supreme something, which was a force from which goodness emanated. Neo-Platonists unified the ideas of Aristotle, the Stoics, some of Pythagoras, mystical ideas, bits of myth and a Platonic reworking of everything in which the body was bad and the spiritual good. If this sounds like Christianity without Christ, that's probably because the Christian synthesis was rather similar. (May the force be with you).

DOCTORS of the CHURCH
Ambrose, Jerome, Gregory, AUGUSTINE

Manichees
Gnostics
Paul
Gospels
Christ
Essenes
Maccabees
Hellenisation
Diaspora
Captivity—the Pentateuch
Prophets
Moses

Neo-Platonists
Christian Platonists
Plotinus
Stoics
Philo
Cynics & Sceptics
Aristotle
Plato
Pythagoreans
Pre-Socratics
Orphic Mysticism

Christianity, like all religions, developed over the years. It was to be a very grand synthesis of many elements, which is probably why it stayed the course so well.

Having absorbed Neo-Platonism and Plotinus, Christianity was to dominate philosophy until the Renaissance. Free thought was only possible if it was Christian free thought.

31

The end of scientific free thinking, the rise of Christian dogma, and the final decline of the Greco-Roman civilization are all symbolized in the life and death of **Hypatia (370-415)**.

Hypatia was the daughter of a mathematician and astronomer at the Alexandrian museum. A Neo-Platonist, but not of the religious variety, she probably held a municipal Chair of Philosophy. Alexandria itself was falling apart from battles between Christians, Jews, and pagans, at a time when the Roman Empire was officially becoming Christian.

As a pagan, a philosopher, a scientist and mathematician, an important political figure and a woman, Hypatia wasn't very popular with the narrow-minded Christian zealots. Probably on the orders of St. Cyril, patriarch of Alexandria, she was dragged from her chariot, stripped naked, cut up alive with sharpened shells, and finally burnt. This is what Christians meant by brotherly love.

From here it was all downhill for philosophy. In 525 Justinian closed the remaining philosophy schools, and what we know as the Dark Ages were under way.

The FALL of the ROMAN EMPIRE & The RISE of CHRISTIANITY

Edward Gibbon gave five major causes for the rise of Christianity:

1. The inflexible and intolerant zeal of the Christians — inherited from Judaism.
2. The idea of a life after death
   (a future reward).
3. The miraculous powers ascribed to the Primitive Church.
   (Aided by reactions to disasters and superstition.)
4. The pure and austere morals of the early Christians.
   (Quite unusual at the time.)
5. The unity and discipline of the developing Christian republic, which became a state within a state in the Roman Empire.

This last, political, factor was undoubtedly the most important. While everything was falling apart around it, the Church pursued a coherent policy.

BY 300 AD THE STIR OF THE GREAT PLAINS — THE HUGE TREKS OF THE SO-CALLED BARBARIANS: HUNS, GOTHS, VANDALS ETC — WAS WELL UNDER WAY.

For the Romans, this was the end of Empire, and thus a bad thing... it was also a bad thing for philosophers — religion replaced thought.

The first great task of the Church was to UNIFY the faith in theory and practice

This meant an organised ritual, over which the clergy presided, and a strictly-enforced morality.

To settle the various debates about Christianity the Council of Nicaea was held in 325AD:

The Council established the **Nicene Creed** in which Father and Son, part of the Trinity, were 'identical in essence'.

The Arians, who denied the Trinity, became the first official heretics.

The Creed led to the first great split in Christendom, between the Eastern and Western churches, based on the two wings of the Empire. This split between Roman Catholic and Greek Orthodox still exists.

In 379 the Emperor Theodosius threw his weight behind the new orthodoxy and the 'catholic' triumph was complete.

The Fathers of the Church

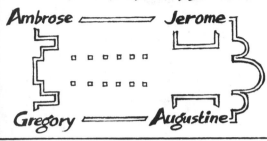

Ambrose ——— Jerome
Gregory ——— Augustine

The four Fathers, or Doctors — apart from Gregory — all lived during the last gasp of the Empire, before the nomadic tribes took over.

St Ambrose

A Roman lawyer, and for a while Governor of Liguria, became Bishop of Milan.

Ambrose insisted on the spiritual supremacy of the Church over everyone, including the Emperor. This was a radical position – going well beyond what Christ had said. Ambrose put the Church before the State and so started a long and bitter debate.

Ambrose wrote plenty of letters, so we know what he argued.

St Jerome

Jerome also strongly supported the setting-up of monasteries. They became an important force in the consolidation of the Church's power.

Jerome was another man of letters, many of which were about how to preserve virginity.

After five years in the desert as a hermit, he went and worked for the Pope, who encouraged him to translate the Bible. It is for this great work, Jerome's Vulgate, that he is remembered. This first translation into Latin became the orthodox version for the Church — a standard text was needed to settle doctrinal disputes.

HEBREW Torah — Latin Vulgate — GREEK Septuagint

St Augustine

(354 – 430)

Born in North Africa of a Christian mother and a pagan father, he lived most of his life there, the last 35 years as Bishop of Carthage.

After a good deal of sinning, which included stealing pears as a child, and frequent trips to the brothels of Carthage as a young man, Augustine eventually dedicated his life to celibacy and wrote his famous spiritual autobiography, the *Confessions*.

Augustine was the only Father who could really be described as a philosopher.

GREAT SAINTS HAVE TO BE GREAT SINNERS

"I FOUND MYSELF IN THE MIDST OF A HISSING CAULDRON OF **LUST** .. I MUDDIED THE STREAM OF FRIENDSHIP WITH THE **FILTH** OF LEWDNESS "

Augustine's vivid sense of sin drove him to discuss its origins at length. He came down strongly on the side of Original Sin, arguing fiercely against the Welsh cleric Pelagius who suggested there was none.
He even puzzled about his own sin as a baby in crying at his mother's breast.
He made an important distinction, however: individuals could sin, but the true Church, as an institution of God, could not.

This proved handy when the Church came to run things and had to deal with heretics.

36

Augustine certainly struggled with ideas, and with himself. This is what sets him apart from the other clerics

THESE TWO WILLS WITHIN ME ONE OLD, ONE NEW, ONE THE SERVANT OF THE **FLESH**, THE OTHER OF THE **SPIRIT**, TORE MY SOUL APART

Augustine was intensely acquisitive of the various scraps of classical learning of his day.
He learnt rhetoric and logic.
He admired the Stoics:

> 'The Scriptures seemed quite unworthy of comparison with the stately prose of Cicero, because I had too much conceit to accept their simplicity.'

He dabbled in Plotinus and the neo-Platonists but was most drawn to the scepticism of the late Academy.
He read Aristotle's categories.
He joined the Manichean sect which was fashionable amongst intellectuals.
He saw his conversion, when it finally came, as a humbling of his intellectual pride, and a dissolution of his will into the will of God:

> 'We are too weak to discover the truth by reason alone.'

Then his problem was to square his old knowledge and his new belief, and show that they were interdependent.

Augustine also had a problem with Time and Creation.
According to Genesis God created the world out of nothing.
But in Greek philosophy there was a strong objection to something being created out of nothing...
And what was God doing before he made heaven and earth?

To this question Augustine rejected the wisecrack:
> 'Preparing HELL for those who pry into mysteries.'

Instead Augustine argued that God is Eternal, and therefore outside time.

Time started for us when the world was created, for God is just there all the time, in an Everlasting Present.

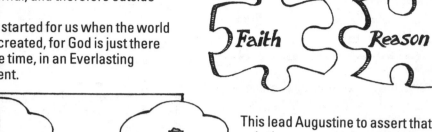

This lead Augustine to assert that only the *present* truly exists. The past exists only as a *present* memory, and the future only as a *present* expectation.

THIS VERY SUBJECTIVE NOTION OF TIME HINTS AT THE WAY DESCARTES WAS TO ARGUE MUCH LATER.

Most important of all Augustine wrote the **CITY of GOD**

Here he developed a Christian view of the past, and began what we call the philosophy of history.
(The notion that history has a discernible pattern.)
After a philosophical interpretation of the Creation as allegory, he posed a City of God and a City of the Devil. One was made of man's virtues, the other of his vices.
The City of God can only be known through the 'infallible authority' of the Church.
If the state wanted to be part of the City, it had to obey the Church.

CITY LIMITS
No Pagans
No Jews

This was to prove a powerful theological weapon in the rise of the Papacy, as was Augustine's view that God had divided everyone up into the elect and the reprobates.

Boethius
(480 - 524)

In the midst of all this Christian argument & religious fervour, **Boethius** stands out like a **Stoic** at a chimpanzee's tea party

A WISE MAN'S VERY DISTRESS IS AN OPPORTUNITY TO STRENGTHEN HIS WISDOM

Philosophia

Condemned to death by the Emperor **Theodoric**, who he **had** hoped to turn into **Plato's** philosopher-king, **Boethius** was sent to prison. There he wrote his famous

"Consolations of Philosophy"

In it "he nowhere finds consolation in any Christian belief", but instead in his guardian, Philosophy, who appears in his cell and promises to *"lead him to true happiness"*.

Although a Christian, he seems to have had little sense of sin and tried to prove that

"vice is never unpunished nor virtue unrewarded"

Much taken with **Plato's** theory of anamnesis, he allows his guardian Philosophy to re-awaken in him his sense of independent fortitude.

Boethius saw himself as the schoolmaster of the West, planning to translate all of Plato and Aristotle. He wasn't very successful at this either and was executed before he got past the first few.

Boethius also set out his answer to the problem of universals, "whether things actually exist or are found only in the mind". This argument ran and ran, but along tracks laid down by the Prisoner. He was the model of a philosopher for the next 1,000 years of lights out.

Boethius shines in his ability to use the disinterested rationality of Greek thought in an era of superstition and mysticism — a true LOVER of WISDOM.

The DARK AGES

Crudely we can say that while everything else fell apart in Europe, the Roman Catholic Church systematically organised itself into the ruling body.

In an age of war and plague the **PAPACY** filled the political vacuum left by the collapse of the Roman Empire.

Wheeling and dealing between Greek emperors, Italian princes, raiding Vandals, warring Lombards and Franks and anyone else who was carving up bits of Europe, the Papacy steadily extended its power.

> SHALL I SAY GRACE OR WILL YOU?

In one deal with the Frank **Pepin** the Pope got the city of Ravenna and the Italian church-lands in exchange for crowning Pepin King in **751.**

The **Byzantine Empire** took exception and forced another split between eastern and western churches. To legitimate the deal a forged document — the **_Donation of Constantine_** — was trumped up. It claimed that Rome and its lands was given to the **Papacy** when **Constantine** shifted the seat of Empire to Constantinople in 312.

The HOLY ROMAN EMPIRE

In the midst of all this disorder, **Pepin's** son, **Charlemagne,** created a brief renaissance.

He whipped the Lombards, made himself King, took over Rome, conquered most of Germany, spread Christianity by sword and fire to Saxony and had himself crowned Emperor by the Pope. His coronation on Christmas Day, **800,** marks the beginning of the

HOLY ROMAN EMPIRE

Charlemagne's grand scheme was a compound of two dreams:

> **The recreation of the imperial rule of the Caesars**
> **The building on earth of St Augustine's City of God**

For a time there were new levels of co-operation between the secular powers and the Papacy.

But after **Charlemagne's** death wars and fights between the Church and the string of **"imitation Caesar"** Emperors returned.

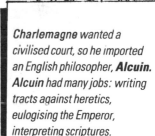

Charlemagne wanted a civilised court, so he imported an English philosopher, **Alcuin.** Alcuin had many jobs: writing tracts against heretics, eulogising the Emperor, interpreting scriptures.

But probably most important, he worked as an elementary school teacher.

(Charlemagne never quite got the hang of writing.)

41

As **Voltaire** said later:
"The HOLY ROMAN EMPIRE was neither HOLY, nor ROMAN, nor an EMPIRE"

The Carolingnian renaissance was soon followed by an 'age of barbarism': feudal enslavement, poverty and ignorance amidst further wars and plagues.

Pope Nicholas I (858-67) strengthened the Papacy by winning all his quarrels, but thereafter it sank into a plaything of the local Roman aristocracy.

The low point came with **John XI** and **John XII.**

John XII, who became Pope at the age of sixteen, "completed the debasement of the Papacy by his **debauched** life and the **orgies** of which the Lateran palace soon became the scene".

No-one can live by Catholicism alone and some-one had to pay for the luxuries of the Papacy, the wars, church-building and the upkeep of monasteries. It was generally the peasants who did the work, of course, and just had to be philosophical about it. They worked the land and someone else generally took some, all or part of what they produced. This was called feudalism, an agriculturally based economic system in which, as Marx said,

"we find everyone dependent, serfs and lords, vassals and suzerains, laymen and clergy"

Slavery generally disappeared in Western Europe after the decline of the Roman Empire and the control of land was the key source of power. Feudalism is generally thought to have evolved out of the Frankish kingdom of the Merovingians, to have accelerated during Carolingian Renaissance and to have reached its 'classic period' during the tenth to the thirteenth centuries. The word feudal comes from 'fief', which refers to a bit of land that was granted (to whoever) in return for services, loyalty and produce. The trade was two-way however and the lord, or the Church, was meant to protect the serf, vassal, peasant or tenant. Thus it was that a complex system grew up in which the law, the ideology, religion and custom all fitted together in what was meant to be a stable system.

Never before or since were ideas and beliefs more closely allied with social and political circumstances.

IRELAND

Ireland managed to preserve a knowledge of Greek culture when elsewhere it was fading in Europe.

Scholars may have fled there to escape Gauls and other raiders. In the 6th to 9th centuries this learning flourished in the Irish monasteries, and because the influence of Rome was slight, it was a learning free of orthodoxy. Unfortunately, apart from the beautiful illuminated manuscripts, little survives of the period.

CHINA

In China the **Tang Dynasty (618-907)** was flourishing. It was a complex civilisation with advanced technology, intensive agriculture and a tightly-knit social organisatoin. Its culture reflected the glories of its new-found prosperity. Its capital, Chang An, was the largest and most civilised city in the world. It was,, says **Obata**, *"a great cosmopolitan city where Syrians, Arabs, Persians, Tartars, Tibetans, Koreans, Japanese and Tonkinese… lived side by side, presenting a remarkable contrast to the ferocious religious and racial strife then prevailing in Europe"*.

The Emperor **Hi-Shih-Min** founded a university and a library with 20,000 volumes. Poetry and painting were at a peak. In the 8th Century the Han Lin Academy, the model for European academies a millenium later, was founded.

THE MUSLIM WORLD

Almost as extraordinary as the rise of Greek civilisation was the rise of Muslim culture in the seventh century.

A slow starter as a prophet, **Mohammed** was forty before he began to preach and fifty-one when he fled Mecca to the rival city Medina in 622. The Hegira, or Flight, marks the beginning of Mohammedanism as a new force in the world.

Mohammed preached a simple monotheism full of the chivalrous Bedouin sentiments of the desert — kindliness, generosity and brotherhood. He abolished the old blood-feuds between Arabs, and showed a practical attitude to trade and property.

Although missionary in outlook, the Moslems gained ascendancy over the weak and disorganised older societies without much bloodshed, and showed a new religious tolerance.

Their own knowledge of irrigation, agriculture and commerce was added to through their conquests. From Syria they learnt of Greek philosophy and Aristotle. From Persia they learnt of Indian culture. From Sanskrit writings they took what we now call 'Arabic' numerals. From China they learnt paper-making.

Muhammed ib Musa al-Khwarazmi published in 830 an influential book *"Algoritmi de numero Indium"* (translated into Latin in the 12th Century). He also produced a work on algebra which was in use in the West up to the 16th Century.

By 1100 the Arabs led the world in their knowledge of astronomy, medicine and chemistry.

Their architecture, art and artefacts were also of great beauty and sophistication.

43

An extraordinary free-thinker who emerged from the Irish monastic tradition was

Johannes Scotus Eriugena
(800-77)

John the Scot, as he was known, was of course an Irishman. Scholar, neo-platonist and pantheist, he must have been born lucky, since he escaped persecution for heresy in his lifetime. Later **Pope Honorius** ordered his books to be burned.

John's main sins were:

Believing in free will — and arguing for it philosophically, not theologically. This was in his **"On Divine Predestination".**

Saying philosophy was as important as religion. Reason and revelation were both sources of truth, but reason was superior. This was terribly wicked — the Church condemned his work as 'Scots porridge'.

Being a pantheist — also very wicked. He said God and the Universe were identical and the Creation was timeless. He thought Genesis had to be read allegorically. Unlike **Augustine** he thought Man was once without sin and punishment not eternal, if still nasty. All this was close to atheism.

His **"On the Division of Nature"** praised Plato's Ideas, divided Nature into four classes and was too clever by half for the Church's liking.

John also translated out of Greek the strange-sounding **Pseudo-Dionysius,** who, 300 years earlier, had tried to fuse neo-platonism and Christianity. *This translation shocked the Pope and his librarian — how could an Irishman understand Greek so well?*

According to Heiric of Auxerre (876):

" Ireland is migrating almost en masse with her crowd of philosophers to our shores "

LATER, THE IRISH THINKERS RE-COLONISED EUROPE

The Arabs

If History moves in mysterious ways, philosophy seems no different. Since the Arabs learnt Greek philosophy through the Syrians, who supported **Aristotle** and not Plato, Aristotle became **THE** Greek philosopher for the Muslim world.

Kindi

Kindi was the first to write in Arabic on philosophy. He translated Plotinus' *"Enneads"*, entitling it *"The Theology of Aristotle"* (confusing, eh? Plotinus' whole system was based on Plato — remember?)

45

Avicenna (980 -1036)

Well-known as the Falasifa who attempted a synthesis between Islam, Plato and Aristotle. Famous also for his writings on medicine and psychology, and his passions for travel, wine and women, **Avicenna** settled as a teacher in Tehran. He wrote an enyclopaedia which was widely-read in the West, and invented a neat Aristotelian catch-phrase:

"Thought brings about the generality of forms."

(Universals exists in men's thoughts, and also in God's understanding. Universals existed before, during and after THINGS — e.g. God has the Idea of a whale before it is created. Once, created, whales partake of the Idea of whaleness. After we've seen a few whales we have a glimmer of the universal 'whale'.)

WHERE'S THE UNIVERSAL WHALE TODAY?

Averroës (1126 - 1198)

Averroës lived in Cordova until he was exiled by the Caliph for not contenting himself with the true faith. He revered **Aristotle**, giving him the status of a prophet, and freeing him from neo-platonist overlays. He believed, as did **Aquinas** later, that God's existence could be proved by reason alone. He argued, like, **Aristotle**, against the immortality of the soul. An orthodox muslim, **Algazel** objected to such views, and claimed in his **"Destruction of the Philosophers"** that all philosophy was bad for you.

Averroës retorted with **"Destruction of the Destruction"** where he argued that all religion was a form of allegorical philosophy.

Maimonides (1135 - 1204)

A Spanish Jew who wrote in Arabic, **Maimonides** also helped transmit **Aristotle** to the West. In Cairo he wrote his famous **"Guide to Wanderers"**. Aimed at the poor souls who had lost their faith under the affliction of philosophy, the book argued that the pursuit of truth was religion itself. He invoked **Aristotle** as an authority on almost everything. These Arabic texts, quickly tranlated into Latin, had an enormous impact on the European clerical scholars. After the intellectual stagnation of the Dark Ages a new energy appeared in the philisophy of the West. Its first expression was **SCHOLASTICISM.**

SCHOLASTICISM got underway as a philosophical school in the 11th Century. It represented the growing strength of the Church in learning and culture, and the newfound interest in ancient philosophy, particularly Aristotle.

*Because knowledge of Aristotle came through the Arabs it was at first suspect and even the greatest scholastic, **Thomas Aquinas** was· initially condemned.*
But the Church soon realised they were on to a good thing — Aquinas was canonised, and eventually, in 1879, his philosophy became the approved teachings of Roman Catholicism.

The Rise of Scholasticism

Scholasticism began to emerge in the 11th Century with the beginnings of a new sense of order after the preceding 400 years of chaos. There was growth and reform in the monasteries, and an increase in the general level of education, even among the laity.

New Orders of monks appeared, opposed to the wealth and worldliness of established monasticism. The **Carthusians**, the **Camaldolese** and the well-known **Cistercians** operated like reforming political parties within the constitution of the Church.

Three things were sorted out amongst the clergy: **simony, concubinage** and **transubstantiation.**
(They all sound like sins — but the last isn't.)
Simony was flogging off positions of power, concubinage the clergy's practice of taking mistresses and transubstantiation the miracle of the mass.

The first two were banned and the last became an article of faith.

The first of the early schoolmen was **Roscelin** (b.1050), who was, by all accounts, neither a very nice person nor a good philosopher. He said that universals were just *"breath of the voice"* or words — mere physical acts.

He also mocked his poor pupil,

Abelard (1079 - 1142)

a much better philosopher.

Famous for his love affair with Helöise, for which he was castrated by Helöise's uncle, he ended his days in a monastery where he confined himself to study.

His best-known work is *"Sic et Non"* or *"Yes and No"* in which he brought the *dialectic* back into fashion. He argued that apart from the Scriptures, the dialectic was the road to the truth and generally good for the mind. He also put forward a complex argument against universals.

More wise monks ..

Part also of the intellectual revival was **Berengar of Tours**.
He argued that reason was more relevant than revelation. he also supported **John the Scot**, which got **John** condemned posthumously, and himself into deep water.

St Peter Damien was much more conventional. In his *"On Divine Omnipotence"* he opposed simony, argued against the newly fashionable dialectic and claimed God could do anything — even change the past!

St Anselm
(1093 - 1109)

Anselm, who became Archbishop of Canterbury, is best known for his **"ontological argument"** for the existence of God. Theologians didn't like it, Aquinas rubbished it later, but it has intrigued philosophers. Anselm claimed God sent him the argument in a vision after breakfast on 13th July 1099 – so it must be true...

It goes like this:
*"We say God is the greatest object of thought. Now if we say something doesn't exist, something else exactly like it, if it **did** exist, just by virtue of existing would be greater. So if God doesn't exist, we could imagine something greater, namely a God that **does** exist. Since we can conceive of this greater God, God himself must exist for otherwise an even greater one would. So God exists."*
What's wrong with that?
Anselm was the last philosopher to remain in the Platonic tradition.

49

St Thomas Aquinas (1225-74)

The "Angelic Doctor"

St Thomas Aquinas was an aristocratic Italian who became a Dominican and studied under one of the leading Aristotelians of the time, **Albertus Magnus.**

The Dominicans were thought to be under the influence of the **Averroists** in Paris, and probably heretical. **Aquinas** set out to make all this Aristotelian influence respectable and was, of course, ultimately successful.

Like **Aristotle** he tried to organise all branches of knowledge into a complete SYSTEM.

His two most important works are: *"Summa contra Gentiles"* and *"Summa Theologiae".*

Here he sets out the full system which was to become the approved philosophy of the Church.

At the heart of his system lies the distinction between *"natural theology"* and *"revealed theology".*

The first comes from the activity of reason and from sense experience, the second from faith, divine grace and the Scriptures. The object of both, however, is the apprehension of God.

This overlap of what **Aquinas** saw as separate areas later produced problems he hadn't dreamed of.

Unwittingly, by his very systematism AQUINAS began to shatter the established identity of GOD & THE WORLD, KNOWLEDGE & REALITY, FAITH & REASON

Summa
APPROVED

Aquinas..

In the **"Summa contra Gentlies"** Aquinas set out to prove to a non-Christian, through natural reason, the importance of Christianity and the existence of God. Before putting his own views he disposed of others that he thought weren't up to scratch.

They were:

1) The self-evident argument

Since we can't **know** the essence of God, we can't **know** he exists. And anyway, since agnostics don't believe in God it *isn't* self-evident.

2) The ontological argument. *(Anselm's argument)*

Firstly, **Aquinas** points out that the idea of God as that *"than which no greater can be thought"* is not generally accepted. Secondly, knowledge of the essence of God is inaccessible to human reason, which relies instead on sense experience. Thirdly, to argue from the idea of God to his existence is wrong — because it's a jump from concepts to existence, from idea to fact.

Aquinas produces five proofs of his own:

1) The argument from Change
Change is everywhere. Someone causes it — so there *must* be a God like **Aristotle's Unmoved Mover**

2) The argument from Causation
Who causes causes? Is there a **First Cause**, itself uncaused? **Aquinas** says there is.

3) The argument from Contingency
How do we account for contingency in nature?
You guessed it — a **Necessary Being**, beyond contingency.

4) The argument from Degrees of Excellence
We notice degrees of excellence in nature. This imples the notion of perfection, which in turn implies what we might call a **Perfect Being**.

5) The argument from Harmony
Aquinas points out that everywhere we look there is "adaptation" or "accord". Fish need to swim so they have fins and tails, dogs need to gnaw bones so they have strong teeth.
We can either say this is merely accident or we can argue for "design" — the manifestation of an **Intelligence** that organises things.
Well, **Aquinas** plumps for the latter.

BIT **SKETCHY** ISN'T IT?

IT'S ONLY A **BEGINNER'S** GUIDE..

There were three other important philosophers who we call schoolmen but who didn't necessarily agree with **Aquinas**, or with each other. They were **Roger Bacon, Duns Scotus** and **William of Occam**.

Roger Bacon
(1214 – 1294)

HOW CAN AQUINAS BE SUCH AN AUTHORITY ON ARISTOTLE WHEN HE CAN'T READ GREEK?

SSH! YOU'LL END UP IN PRISON

Roger Bacon is certainly the best known of the schoolmen today and this is because he is seen as having first laid stress on the importance of science and in particular of experimentation (although some Greeks had as well). Because of his rather free-thinking attitudes he got himself into trouble with the authorities and when he openly attacked clerical ignorance he got himself into prison for fourteen years. He wrote on many things including geography, alchemy and mathematics, he discussed perspective and even suggested that one could learn things from the heathen, in particular the Arabs. In his "Opus Majus" he argued that there were four causes of ignorance, arguments that are still sound today. They were:

1) Appeals to an unsuited authority
2) The undue influence of custom
3) The opinions of the unlearned crowd
4) Displays of wisdom that simply covered up ignorance.

After **Aristotle, Bacon** thought Avicenna the most important philosopher and in this he was quite different to other scholastics. He gained his empirical bent from **Aquinas**, his encyclopaedic leanings from the Arabs and his contempt for most of his colleagues, particularly translators, from we know not where.

Duns Scotus
(1270— 1308)

Duns Scotus was a Franciscan who, like his namesake **John the Scot**, was probably Irish. He was also interested in evidence and held that there were three classes of things that can be known without proof:

1) Principles known by themselves
2) Things known by experience
3) Our actions themselves

It was taken for granted that these things could only ultimately be known through divine revelation.

Duns Scotus also discussed the "principle of individuation" which was one of the more important problems of scholastic philosophy. The basic problem is, how do you tell one thing apart from another? Like other things in philosophy this seems simple but the more you think about it the more complicated it gets. **Duns Scotus** held that there was no difference between *being* and *essence* and that therefore it was *form* that distinguished one thing from another, and not *matter*. Against **Aquinas** Duns Scotus defended the Immaculate Conception and practically everybody seems to have agreed with him.

The word "DUNCE" comes from his followers, called DUNSES, because they opposed classical studies!

What is **scholasticism**?
Here's a rough definition. (Remember it's all essentially about God, but very complex in details.)

- 1) An acceptance of the prevailaing catholic orthodoxy
- 2) Within this orthodoxy, an acceptance of **Aristotle** as a greater thinker than **Plato**
- 3) A recognition that **Aristotle** and **Plato** disagreed about the notion of universals — and that this was a vital question to resolve
- 4) Giving prominence to 'dialectical' thinking and syllogistic reasoning
- 5) An acceptance of the distinction between 'natural' and 'revealed' theology. (Rather like the older distinction between reason and revelation.)
- 6) A tendency to dispute everything at length. (Some people called it word-play.)

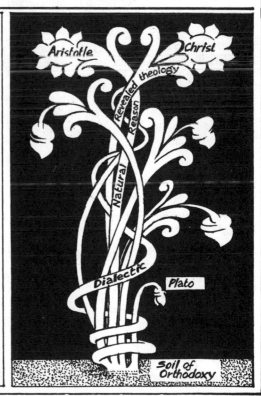

William of Occam
(1290 – 1349)

William of Occam was by common consent the greatest of scholastic logicians and originally the pupil of **Duns Scotus**, who he later disagreed with. He also disagreed with the Pope over transubstantiation and over the Pope's insistence that a group known as the Spirituals should accept the ownership of property and give up their vow of poverty. This led to **William** being excommunicated in 1328 and taking refuge with the **Emperor**. By this time the battle between the Pope and Emperor had really become a battle between France and Germany. The Holy Roman Empire had practically ceased to exist. Whilst under the protection of the Emperor **William** wrote several important political tracts. In them he argued for less secular power for the Church and for more democracy. These were the kinds of ideas that were eventually to lead to the Renaissance and the Reformation.

In philosophy **William** is famous for his invention of *"Occam's razor"* which is supposed to have put an end to all the pedantry of scholasticism. He is supposed to have said,:
> *"entities are not to be multiplied without necessity"*

in fact what he said was:
> *"It is vain to do with more what can be done with fewer"*

by which he meant that the simplest form of statement is superior to endless hypotheses.

More importantly **Occam** attempted to bring some rigour back to the study of logic. He felt that **Aristotle** had been misunderstood by many people and that this had led logic and the theory of knowledge to fall into the grip of metaphysics and theology. Logic, **Occam** argued, is the analysis of scientific terms whereas science itself is about things. Logic treats universals and is concerned with terms and concepts not physical states. This is all very modern and Occam made little attempt to square these ideas with the standard notion of the divine presence which ordered all systems. So although **Occam** agreed with **Aquinas** on many things he actually laid the seeds for the collapse of the great mediaeval system of philosophy.

Umberto Eco's "Name of the Rose" gives a vivid picture of this period of emerging empiricism

A Mediaeval World-View

Citadel

City walls

Beyond the city walls

The mediaeval obsession with structure and with allegory is clear from the world-view of the 13th century poet **Alanus.**

There is a place for everything, and everything is in its proper place.

The **social structure** of King, Barons and Commons is pictured by the Citadel, those *within* the City Walls, and those *without* the City Walls.

This triad has a **theological** correspondence of God-Angels-Mankind.

King (God)

Barons (Angels)

Commons (Mankind)

The **individual** soul also has a triadic structure (borrowed from **Plato**) of Head (Reason)-Heart (Emotion)-Belly (Appetite).

So the whole picture is:

God	King	Head
Angels	Barons	Heart
Mankind	Commons	Belly

And the picture is extended to **cosmology**.

God exists in the Empyrean, beyond the sphere of fixed stars. In the space between there and the sphere of the moon's orbit live the nine orders of angels. Furthest from God, on earth, is suffering mankind.

(The three nesting spheres have to be imagined turned inside out.) Holding the whole thing together: the great binding ideas of feudalism — HONOUR and LOYALTY.

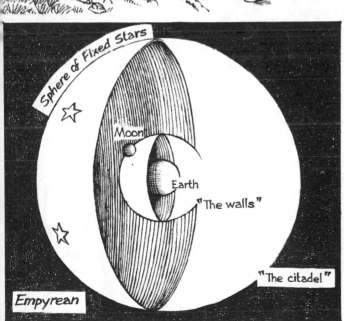

Sphere of Fixed Stars

Moon

Earth

"The walls"

"The citadel"

Empyrean

John Wycliffe
(1320 – 1384)

THE POPE IS THE ANTI-CHRIST!

CAN YOU SMELL BURNING?

WYCLIFFE was of the most unlikely, and probably most unwilling, radicals of all time. He was a local priest, a doctor of theology from Oxford and well into middle age before the corruption of the Church forced him into criticism of the Papacy. He was the last of the scholastics, although more of a Platonist than an Aristotelean, and argued that the world as it is was the only possible world since God ordained it.

His descent into radicalism began in 1376 when he gave a course of lectures at Oxford *'On Civil Dominion'*. He argued that righteousness alone conferred the right to property and power and that therefore corrupt, rich ecclesiastics had no such rights. He went further and pointed out that Christ and the early apostles had no property and that the clergy shouldn't have any either.

This didn't go down very well with a rich church that sent a huge tribute off to Rome every year but the English government liked the idea. The bishops tried to condemn him at trial but **WYCLIFFE** was protected by Royalty and the masses.

Wycliffe kept getting more radical as he got older and he eventually denied transubstantiation. This and the peasants revolt of 1381, which people took as being inspired by him, could have got him into serious trouble but he conveniently died in 1384. His followers, the Lollards, were quickly stamped out and after he had been condemned his bones were dug up and burnt. The seeds of revolt that **Wycliffe** sowed spread as far as Bohemia where, under Huss, they thrived and, despite persecution, lasted until the Reformation.

Huss wasn't so lucky: he was burnt alive

Wycliffe went further and raised issues that were to dominate Europe for the next four centuries. He argued that the King was God's vicar and the Church subject to him, that the Church should concentrate on spiritual matters and that the Pope was not only a good thing, but the Anti-Christ. He also translated the Vulgate into English, a move into a national language that was often repeated during the Renaissance and gave many people beside the clergy access to the Bible.

SCHOLASTICISM is often seen as a bad joke. But even its wickedest critic, the Renaissance satirist **RABELAIS**, understood the importance of the mediaeval disputations

> A MOST SUBTLE QUESTION: WHETHER A CHIMERA BOMBINATING IN A VACUUM CAN DEVOUR SECOND INTENTIONS

And the disputes **did** sharpen the linguistic tools for the RENAISSANCE...

The great era of feudal synthesis was breaking up, the Church was everywhere resented, the papacy had little authority after the farce of the **Great Schism**, when there were three Popes for a while, and the strings of nationalism were further undermining the Papacy. In Italy the rise of a rich, educated commercial class, and the rise of democratic tendencies in increasingly powerful city states, led to a new, more critical, even humanist outlook.

The Middle Ages, with its asceticism, piety, thoughts only of the after-life, and theological philosophy was coming to an END

Mediaeval Postscript
The French Duc du Berry was so enamoured of the splendours of his High Gothic life-style he commissioned an Illustrated Book of Hours by the Limbourg brothers, and then bankrupted himself buying the rare lapis lazuli from which the painters derived their brilliant blues

The beginnings of the modern world, the growth of capitalist society, came out of the economic structure of feudal society and the transition was long, bloody and complicated. The rise of great commercial city-states in Northern Italy during the 14th and 15th centureis, and the rise of a rich commercial class who were educated, political and secular, set this process in train. The corruptness of the church, the horrors of the Inquisition and the beginnings of nationalism combined to undermine the Catholic synthesis and led first to the interlude we know as the **Renaissance**, and then the **Reformation** and the **Counter-Reformation**.

With the middle ages died the spirit of scholastic philosophy and in its place there arose a new sense of critical inquiry that looked straight back to the Greeks. The foundations of modern philosophy and science were laid during the 15th and 16th centuries as the world was opened up both to new thought and to new explorers.
How did all this happen?

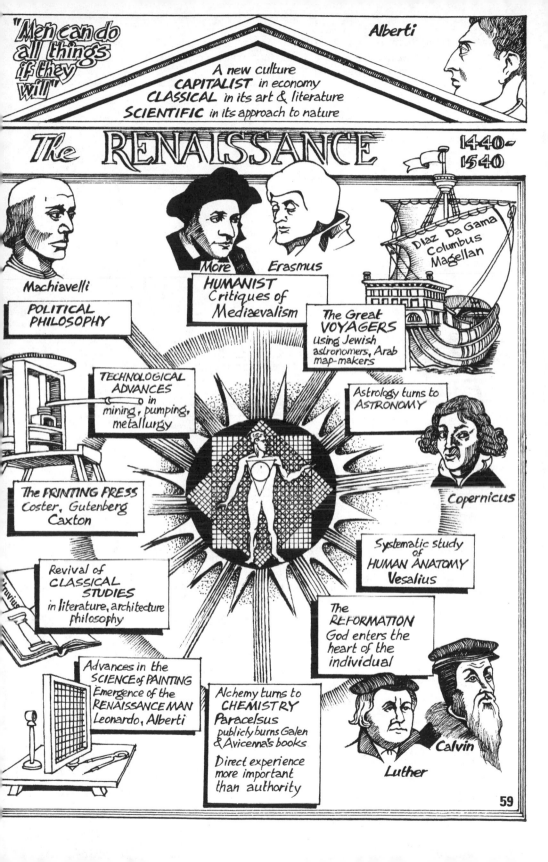

"Men can do all things if they will"

Alberti

A new culture
CAPITALIST in economy
CLASSICAL in its art & literature
SCIENTIFIC in its approach to nature

The RENAISSANCE 1440-1540

Machiavelli

POLITICAL PHILOSOPHY

More   Erasmus

HUMANIST Critiques of Mediaevalism

Diaz   Da Gama   Columbus   Magellan

The Great **VOYAGERS** Using Jewish astronomers, Arab map-makers

TECHNOLOGICAL ADVANCES in mining, pumping, metallurgy

Astrology turns to **ASTRONOMY**

Copernicus

The **PRINTING PRESS** Coster, Gutenberg Caxton

Systematic study of **HUMAN ANATOMY** Vesalius

Revival of **CLASSICAL STUDIES** in literature, architecture philosophy

The **REFORMATION** God enters the heart of the individual

Advances in the **SCIENCE OF PAINTING** Emergence of the **RENAISSANCE MAN** Leonardo, Alberti

Alchemy turns to **CHEMISTRY** Paracelsus publicly burns Galen & Avicenna's books

Direct experience more important than authority

Luther   Calvin

59

The rise of humanism and the rejection of the church led to the great explosion of art and literature of the Renaissance but it was all a bit, well, anarchistic. (The puritans would probably have said immoral if they'd been around — but they come a bit later.)

The person who thought through all these changes and incidentially kicked off political philosophy was the well known

Machiavelli
(1469 – 1527)

Unlike all of the mediaeval philosophers, **Machiavelli** made no attempt to bring God into his thinking, except to point out that pretending to be pious was a good thing to keep the masses happy. What **Machiavelli** was interested in was

Political Power

Caesar Borgia, Machiavelli's ideal Prince, relaxing (Above), and ready for action (below)

and how to get it, keep it and use it. He had plenty of examples around him in 15th century Italy where principalities changed hands every five minutes and treachery was an impolite word for changing your mind.

Most people would pretend they ruled by divine right, hereditary necessity or the blessing of the Church. Machiavelli was just concerned to analyse how anyone could grab power, justify it and then hang on to it. Many people think this shows how totally cynical he was, but it was probably more realistic than anyone likes to admit, even today.

AS A PRINCE MUST BE ABLE TO ACT JUST LIKE A BEAST, HE SHOULD LEARN FROM THE **FOX** & THE **LION** ONE HAS TO BE A FOX TO RECOGNISE TRAPS AND A LION TO FRIGHTEN OFF WOLVES

Machiavelli's two books *"The Prince"* and *"The Discourses"* offer different solutions as to what is politically best, in different circumstances.

In *"The Prince"* Machiavelli argued that in a corrupt world a strong government was necessary, or in other words a dictator. This was probably meant to impress the Medicis who ruled Florence at the time, but they didn't give him a job so he just had to carry on writing. Looking at the corruption around him Machiavelli came to the conclusion that in politics the means of achieving things had to be corrupt also.

Or in fact any means was acceptable as long as it was effective.

This debate about ends and means is central to all political and moral philosophy and no-one else has ever stated it so baldly

HOW DO I BECOME A STRONG RULER?

If you want to be a strong and effective ruler then you can have a double standard of behaviour, one for yourself and one for the people. It is also necessary to be cunning as a fox and fierce as a lion and "to be a great feigner and dissembler".

All this may sound wicked but it is really just an empirical statement of what actually goes on in politics.

In *"The Discourses"* Machiavelli was more moderate and argued that a republic with a democratic constitution would be the best thing. He also suggesetd that the important goals for a nation were; independence, security and a well-ordered constitution.

EVER TRIED MODELLING?

ALL I DID WAS TRANSLATE POLITICS INTO THE VERNACULAR, GIVE THEM A SECULAR, SCIENTIFIC BASIS & LAY THE FOUNDATIONS OF MODERN POLITICAL PHILOSOPHY

61

The effects of the Renaissance spread northwards & produced two figures in whom the new spirit of humanism, scepticism & the love of classical literature were obvious. They were friends, disliked scolasticism and thought the Church should be reformed.

The New Humanism

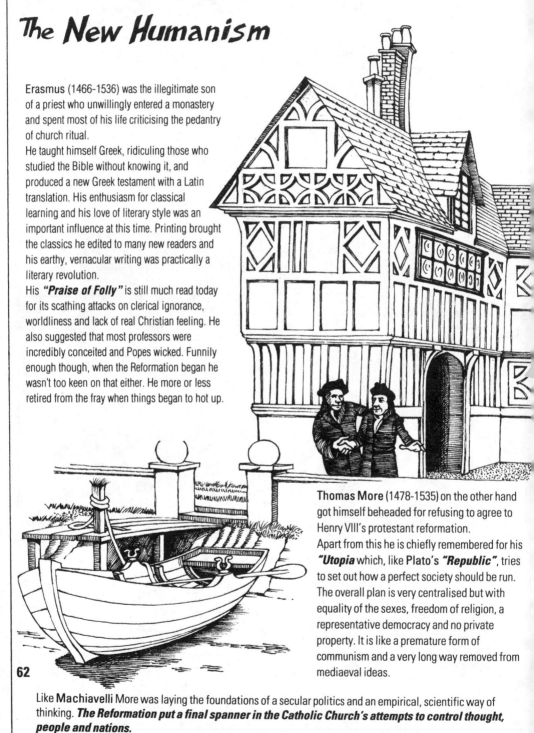

Erasmus (1466-1536) was the illegitimate son of a priest who unwillingly entered a monastery and spent most of his life criticising the pedantry of church ritual.

He taught himself Greek, ridiculing those who studied the Bible without knowing it, and produced a new Greek testament with a Latin translation. His enthusiasm for classical learning and his love of literary style was an important influence at this time. Printing brought the classics he edited to many new readers and his earthy, vernacular writing was practically a literary revolution.

His **"Praise of Folly"** is still much read today for its scathing attacks on clerical ignorance, worldliness and lack of real Christian feeling. He also suggested that most professors were incredibly conceited and Popes wicked. Funnily enough though, when the Reformation began he wasn't too keen on that either. He more or less retired from the fray when things began to hot up.

Thomas More (1478-1535) on the other hand got himself beheaded for refusing to agree to Henry VIII's protestant reformation.

Apart from this he is chiefly remembered for his **"Utopia** which, like **Plato's "Republic"**, tries to set out how a perfect society should be run. The overall plan is very centralised but with equality of the sexes, freedom of religion, a representative democracy and no private property. It is like a premature form of communism and a very long way removed from mediaeval ideas.

62

Like **Machiavelli** More was laying the foundations of a secular politics and an empirical, scientific way of thinking. *The Reformation put a final spanner in the Catholic Church's attempts to control thought, people and nations.*

The Reformation

Wittenberg Echo

UNKNOWN MONK in CHURCH OUTRAGE

LIST OF COMPLAINTS HAMMERED TO DOOR

95 THESES ATTACK CHURCH CORRUPTION

SECULAR PRINCES BACK BREAKAWAY

MULTI-NATIONAL PAPACY BOSSES FIGHT FOR GRACE-OF-GOD MONOPOLY

Martin Luther
(1483-1546)

WHATEVER YOUR HEART CLINGS TO AND CONFIDES IN, THAT IS **REALLY** YOUR GOD

" THE SOLITARY MONK WHO SHOOK THE WORLD "

In philosophical terms Luther's arguments were backward-looking, deriving from **William of Occam and Augustine**, although their implications were revolutionary.

His central doctrine was justification through **faith,** and not through **works.**

He held the authority of the BIBLE to be supreme over Church tradition. Priests were reviled, and the whole paraphernalia of purgatory, masses, robes, graven images and Papal indulgences was to be swept away.

Luther also argued forcefully for predestination and **St Paul's** notion of sin.

Man's terrible predicament could be solved only by faith, not reason.

Although Luther insisted that men must obey their rulers at all times, others took PROTESTANTISM in more radical directions.

John Calvin
(1509 – 64)

In Geneva **Calvin** created a protestant city-state based on his *"Institutes of the Christian Religion."*

Predestination was again a central doctrine but civil life was organised in an egalitarian way. Calvin's radicalism later gave rise to presbyterianism and congregationalism and influenced the **Pilgrim Fathers** in America.

Zwingli
(1484 – 1531)

In Zurich **Zwingli** attacked the debased monasticism and challenged the role of the priesthood. He went further, and denied transubstantiation – in the mass the bread and wine stayed plain bread and wine!

The Catholic Church's response was
the Counter - Reformation

The Church partly reformed itself, counter-attacked against protestanism and established new Orders, particularly the Jesuits. **Doctrine was reformed and discipline restored at the Council of Trent (1543-63)**

In an era of religious war, Catholic princes also fought the new protestant states

PAPIST!

PRODDY DOG!

The Counter-Reformation slowed the spread of Protestantism but did little for
PHILOSOPHY...

St Ignatius of Loyola
(1491 – 1556)

An ex-soldier, the Spaniard **Ignatius** formed his **Society of Jesus** along military lines

The new Jesuit Order produced strenuous fighters of heresy, vigorous missionaries, and created the best schools in Christendom

What has all this got to do with philosophy?

Well, science has always been connected with philosophy in one way or another, and in the 17th Century advances in scientific thinking started off what we call *"the modern world"* and *"modern philosophy"*.

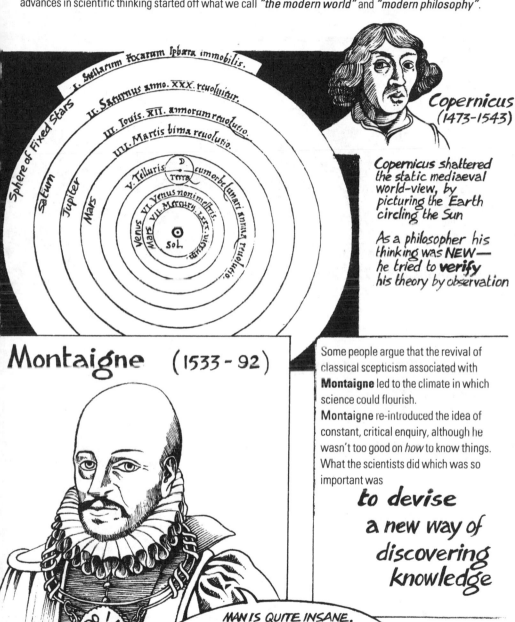

Copernicus (1473-1543)

Copernicus shattered the static mediaeval world-view, by picturing the Earth circling the Sun

As a philosopher his thinking was NEW— he tried to **verify** his theory by observation

Montaigne (1533 - 92)

Some people argue that the revival of classical scepticism associated with **Montaigne** led to the climate in which science could flourish.

Montaigne re-introduced the idea of constant, critical enquiry, although he wasn't too good on *how* to know things.

What the scientists did which was so important was

to devise a new way of discovering knowledge

WHAT DO I KNOW?

MAN IS QUITE INSANE. HE WOULDN'T KNOW HOW TO CREATE A MAGGOT, AND HE CREATES GODS BY THE DOZEN

65

The Rise of Bourgeois Science   1540-1650

Although the centre of culture & learning was Italy, the new **economic** centre of Europe shifted to Holland, England & Northern France, where traders and manufacturers were linked to expanding sea-routes. The first blast-furnaces for pig-iron were built, and the coal to fire them was mined more deeply.

The technology of **navigation**, **gunnery**, **pumping** and **hydraulics** improved dramatically.

A new breed of inventors appeared, and following them the first **experimental philosophers**, or scientists.

Galileo Galilei

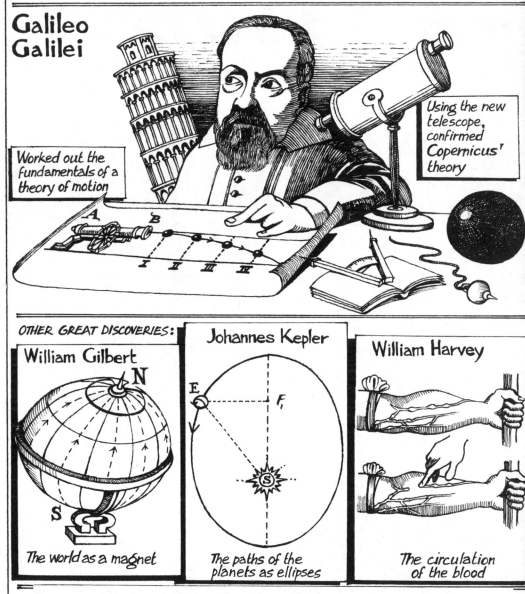

Worked out the fundamentals of a theory of motion

Using the new telescope, confirmed Copernicus' theory

OTHER GREAT DISCOVERIES:

William Gilbert

The world as a magnet

Johannes Kepler

The paths of the planets as ellipses

William Harvey

The circulation of the blood

The two great and hard-won discoveries of the rotation of the planets and the circulation of the blood were established by 1642, the year **Galileo** died and **Newton** was born.

The classical world-picture of Aristotle had gone

Francis Bacon
(1561 – 1626)

A new curiosity was born that produced new knowledge.

Philosophy got left behind a bit until **Sir Francis Bacon** flattened what he called the "degenerate" teachings of the Schoolmen and attacked the general stagnation of learning.

Bacon was interested in discovering ideas that might be useful.

In his **Advancement of Learning** (1605) he argued for natural history, scientific method and the use of knowledge to advance man's estate. He also tried to develop a more materialistic philosophy which went back to Democritus and which aimed to replace the dominant Aristotelian and Platonic traditions.

He is credited with the slogan

IF A MAN WILL BEGIN WITH CERTAINTIES, HE SHALL END IN DOUBTS; BUT IF HE WILL BE CONTENT TO BEGIN WITH DOUBTS, HE SHALL END IN CERTAINTIES

" *Knowledge is Power* "

by which he meant *practical knowledge.*

WE ARE MUCH BEHOLDEN TO **MACHIAVEL** & OTHERS, THAT WRITE WHAT MEN **DO** AND NOT WHAT THEY **OUGHT** TO DO

FAIN WOULD I CLIMB, YET FEAR I TO FALL

Having been Lord Chancellor of England he wasn't afraid of large gestures. "I want," he said, "the total reconstruction of the sciences, arts and all human knowledge."

In searching for knowledge about the world and nature **Bacon** laid great stress on **experimentation** & **observation**.

He tried to put forward a new method of acquiring knowledge, but thought scientific knowledge came simply from endless experimenting.

Bacon wanted to check his conclusions with his observations, which is very modern, but he misunderstood the need for a good experiment to have first a good hypothesis.

However, his *"Advancement of Learning"* clearly marks the end of the old and the beginning of the new, scientific world.

IF HE'D HAD AN HYPOTHESIS ABOUT THE EFFECT OF COLD ON PEOPLE AS WELL AS CHICKENS HE MIGHT HAVE LIVED TO WRITE MORE OF MY PLAYS

Francis Bacon even died for science in the course of an experiment. He was stuffing a chicken with snow, to see if freezing would stop decay, caught a chill, and died from it.

SCIENCE COMES OF AGE
1650–1690

Principia Mathematica "The Bible of the New Science"

Isaac Newton

Using his new mathematical tool, the calculus, **Newton** linked together **Galileo's** mechanics, **Kepler's** planetary laws, & **Gilbert's** theory of attraction into a grand universal scheme.

Simple equations bound the movements of the remotest celestial bodies to the fall of an apple on earth.

*His picture of the **mechanical universe**, so precise in detail, so apparently perfect, was not challenged until **Einstein**, and still dominates the popular imagination.*

Vacuum Pump

Robert Boyle
Returning to the atomism of Democritus, Boyle established the basic physics of gases.

Robert Hooke
A great practical experimenter, Hooke was the "eyes and hands" of the Royal Society, the new Institution for the new natural philosophers

Breakthroughs came in optics and **Leeuwenhoek**, using the microscope, discovered the tiny world of bacteria and spermatozoa

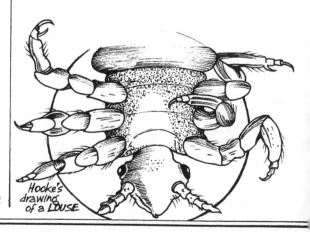

Hooke's drawing of a LOUSE

68

Thomas Hobbes
(1588 ~ 1679)

As everybody knows **Hobbes** wrote *"Leviathan"* and said that life in the state of nature was *"solitary, poor, nasty, brutish and short"*. Despite this, he lived a long life with lots of friends and died happy at the age of 91.

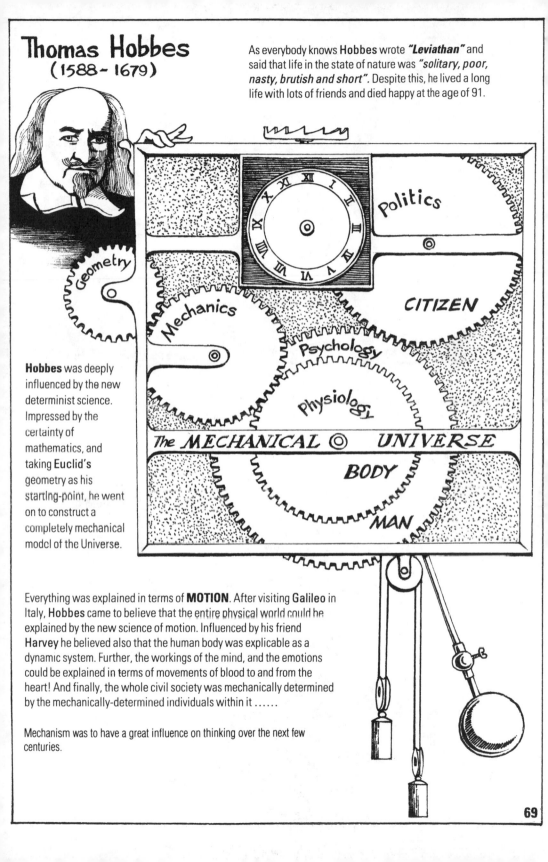

Hobbes was deeply influenced by the new determinist science. Impressed by the certainty of mathematics, and taking **Euclid's** geometry as his starting-point, he went on to construct a completely mechanical model of the Universe.

Geometry
Mechanics
Politics
CITIZEN
Psychology
Physiology
The *MECHANICAL* ◎ *UNIVERSE*
BODY
MAN

Everything was explained in terms of **MOTION**. After visiting **Galileo** in Italy, **Hobbes** came to believe that the entire physical world could be explained by the new science of motion. Influenced by his friend **Harvey** he believed also that the human body was explicable as a dynamic system. Further, the workings of the mind, and the emotions could be explained in terms of movements of blood to and from the heart! And finally, the whole civil society was mechanically determined by the mechanically-determined individuals within it ......

Mechanism was to have a great influence on thinking over the next few centuries.

René Descartes

(1596–1650)

THE FATHER OF MODERN PHILOSOPHY

Handy Labels

SO WHO WAS THE MOTHER?

The son of a French councillor in Brittany, **Descartes** was educated at the Jesuit college of La Flèche, where he was impressed by the certainty and precision of mathematics. After an extended tour of Europe, and some years as a soldier, he settled in Holland.

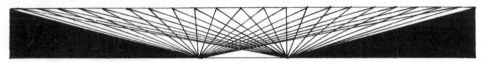

Descartes started out full of scepticism but really wanted some certainty in life. This led him to reject everything he'd been taught and to look for a basis of certainty in his own rational powers.
God, the Church, Aristotle, all previous philosophers and even ancient literature were ditched in the search for rational principles from which to construct a secure system of knowledge.

ALL I'M SAYING IS THAT ALL PAST PHILOSOPHY IS WITHOUT FOUNDATION UNTIL WE'VE EXAMINED ITS PREMISES, AND SHOWN A METHOD OF ADVANCING FROM THEM

IS THAT ALL?

IN FACT I HAD A DREAM ON NOVEMBER 10, 1619, WHICH CONVINCED ME THAT **TRUE KNOWLEDGE** MUST COME FROM **HUMAN REASON** ALONE

Unlike other people, Descartes seems to have dreamed in a systematic & recallable way...

WASN'T HE GOOD AT MATHS?

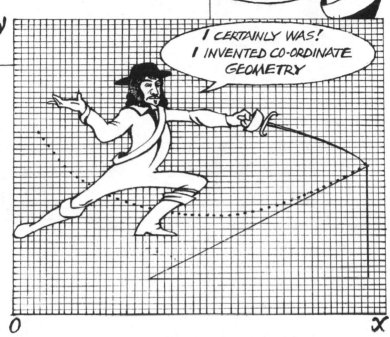

y

I CERTAINLY WAS! I INVENTED CO-ORDINATE GEOMETRY

0

x

What about the philosophy?   The two most important books are:

PHILOSOPHICAL PROPS

"Discourse on Method" (1637) & the *"Meditations"* (1642) **Descartes** tells of a day he spent alone by a stove in Germany when he was still a soldier, and how, little by little, he came upon his whole system of *"Cartesian doubt"*.

CLEAR & DISTINCT IDEAS

FOR MICE

First, he outlined four rules:

Never accept anything except clear and distinct ideas

Divide each problem into as many parts as are needed to solve it

Order your thoughts from the simple to the complex

Always check thoroughly for oversights

Then, sticking to his rules:

Or, in Latin: **COGITO ERGO SUM**

Descartes was so pleased with this discovery he wrote: *"I judged that I could receive it without scruple as the first principle of the philosophy that I sought."*

This led **Descartes** to suppose that the essence of being was thinking, and that the mind was separate from the body.

See later...

All **Descartes** had however was his idea of a **thinking thing**. He couldn't show it could know about the outside world.

To show that he wasn't being deceived, he needed to prove the existence of **God**.

See later...

Next, Descartes considered a lump of bee's-wax.

IT HAS A CERTAIN TASTE, SMELL, COLOUR, SHAPE AND SIZE: IT IS HARD, COLD & EASILY HANDLED

I PUT IT BY THE FIRE AND EVERYTHING CHANGES. THE WAX PERSISTS, BUT IS DIFFERENT. THEREFORE, I KNOW THE WAX THROUGH THE MIND, NOT THE IMAGINATION OR THE SENSES

IN OTHER WORDS, ALL KNOWLEDGE OF EXTERNAL THINGS IS IN THE MIND.

ISN'T THAT A BIT SOLIPSISTIC?

AND DOESN'T IT JUST PROVE THAT ONLY I EXIST, NOT THE OUTSIDE WORLD?

73

YEP, which is why Descartes had to prove God's existence, since God could be the only guarantee that:

1) *Our clear and distinct ideas are true*
2) *We are not being tricked by a wicked demon*

Descartes was happy enough to use a version of **Anselm's** ontological proof, and to argue that the idea of a perfect God must have a cause. Since we are a pretty hopeless lot, it couldn't be us, so **God** must be the cause of *our* idea of *his* perfection.

NEAT—BUT ISN'T IT A BIT CIRCULAR?

Once he'd proved God exists, everything else was downhill:

SO OUR BODY MUST EXIST, EVEN IF IT IS DIFFERENT FROM THE MIND

SO OUR IDEA OF THE OUTSIDE WORLD MUST BE TRUE

SO GOD EXISTS

I EXIST

Which brings us back to the **mind-body problem.** Having said the mind and the body were separate, **Descartes** then had to explain how they worked together in seemingly perfect unison.

Descartes came to the slighlty odd, if logically neat, conclusion that the mind and the body operated like two clocks keeping perfect time.

YOU'RE SLOW!

BODY

YOU'RE FAST!

MIND

Here is a picture of Descartes picturing the MIND picturing the physical world....

The MIND

This **DUALISM** is inherent in all Descartes' thinking and stems from his distinction between THOUGHT and EXTENSION. Because he was convinced that **thinking** had its own principle of motion and that **things** had a separate physical notion he concluded that animals were automata and that the human body acted in a mechanical way.

His follower **GEULINCX** took all this to its logical conclusion and argued that there are two parallel worlds, and that God wound them up at the beginning of time. These DETERMINIST ideas were to have a long influence.

A determined philosopher

LATE AGAIN MR DESCARTES

SWEDISH ALGEBRA

In a rather determinist fashion **Descartes** went off to Sweden to instruct Queen Christina in 1649. She insisted on him teaching her at 5 in the morning. Like all good philosophers he preferred staying in bed till late, and the shock of early rising and the cold killed him within a few months!

Another philosopher greatly influenced by the determinist ideas of the time, and by **Descartes'** rationalism, was

Baruch Spinoza
(1632 – 77)

IT IS OF THE NATURE OF MIND TO PERCEIVE THINGS FROM A CERTAIN *TIMELESS* POINT OF VIEW

Born of Portuguese Jewish parents who had fled from persecution in Spain, he lived in Amsterdam until forced out by those who hated his free thinking. His synagogue excommunicated him, an attempt was made to assassinate him, and orthodox Christians disliked him for what was seen as atheism.

In fact **Spinoza** was one of those rare philosophers who not only believed what he said but acted upon it. He even refused a chair of philosophy at Heidelberg because it was an official position, and that implied accepting official ideas and limitations.

He was by all accounts an honest, noble and courteous man.

Naturally this led to his being attacked by almost everybody, even after he was dead.

His major work, the **"ETHICS"**, was not published during his lifetime, and his other books, the snappily-titled **"Tractatus Theologico-Politicus"** and the **"Tractatus Politicus"** weren't as influential.

Like Descartes **Spinoza** believed that by following the method of geometry we could produce exact knowledge of the real world.

He took it further than Descartes, however, and tried to construct a **GEOMETRY OF PHILOSOPHY**

WHAT'S THAT?

"See the World in its fullness"

A SYSTEM OF DEFINITIONS & AXIOMS LEADING TO PROPOSITIONS THAT *DEMONSTRATE* HOW REALITY WORKS

76

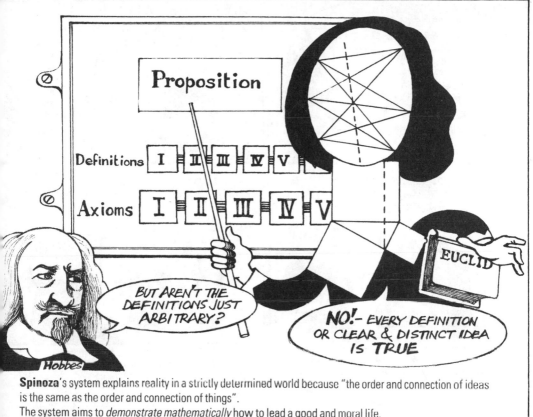

Definitions I II III IV V

Axioms I II III IV V

BUT AREN'T THE DEFINITIONS JUST ARBITRARY?

Hobbes

NO! – EVERY DEFINITION OR CLEAR & DISTINCT IDEA IS TRUE

Spinoza's system explains reality in a strictly determined world because "the order and connection of ideas is the same as the order and connection of things".
The system aims to *demonstrate mathematically* how to lead a good and moral life.

THERE IS ONLY **ONE** SUBSTANCE: "*Deus sive Natura*" – **GOD** OR **NATURE** GOD AND THE COSMOS ARE ONE AND THE SAME

ISN'T THAT **PANTHEISM?**

WELL, YES, BUT IT'S A UNIFYING SCIENTIFIC PRINCIPLE, NOT MYSTICISM

WHAT ABOUT THE SEPARATION OF **MIND & BODY?**

MIND & MATTER ARE JUST ATTRIBUTES OF THE SINGLE SUBSTANCE

77

descartes

Spinoza, with rare intellectual honesty, worked out the inevitable logic of his idea of God and substance, producing a complete description of man, nature and the world. He made his living by grinding lenses, and his enemies by being noble and unambitious.

He truly believed virtue was its own reward: *"There cannot be too much joy: it is always good."*

Spinoza was clearly too much of a good thing, so the next major philosopher to come along was the brilliant, ambitious, pragmatic, orthodox opportunist

Gottfried Wilhelm
Leibniz
(1646 – 1716)

Philosopher in search of a patron

Leibniz was probably the supreme intellect of his age, writing prodigiously on many subjects, as well as inventing the differential calculus. That he was slightly contradictory can be seen from the fact that most of what he pbulished while alive was designed to appeal to the Royalty to whom he attached himself, and was reactionary and shallow, and what he left unpublished was more often profound, original and philosophically important.

In public Leibniz propounded the *"principle of the best"*, which, amongst other things, argued that God has created the best possible world. *This* Leibniz was caricatured in **Voltaire's** *"Candide"* as Dr. Panglos.

Instead of Spinoza's ONE substance, Leibniz proposed an *INFINITY* of infinitesimal simple substances or **MONADS**

$$\frac{d\frac{v}{y}}{} = \frac{v\,dy + y\,dv}{yy}$$

Each MONAD is different, and mirrors the entire Universe, but is not located in space or time...

Monads have no windows by which anything goes in or out

Each MONAD is immaterial, and has a soul...

Monads can't interact with each other

The MONADS appear to act together only because of a pre-established harmony ordained by God

I'LL SUE THE AUTHORS!
WHAT ABOUT MY WORK ON THE METAPHYSICAL PROOFS OF GOD'S EXISTENCE, THE PROBLEM OF EVIL, THE SUBJECT-PREDICATE RELATION, A UNIVERSAL SYMBOLIC LANGUAGE, LOGIC, THE LAW OF CONTRADICTION, HISTORY, JURISPRUDENCE, KINETICS, CHEMISTRY, GEOLOGY & MECHANICS?

While scientific, determinist and rationalist ideas were sweeping Europe an Italian professor of history was quietly sowing the seeds of another intellectual revolution.

Giambattista Vico (1688 – 1744)

was outlining a highly original idea about knowledge and historial enquiry.

THE BROAD OUTLINES OF HISTORY CAN BE KNOWN IN A GENERAL WAY

Initially influenced by **Descartes**, **Vico** came to reject his thinking — particularly the 'cogito ergo sum', the belief in God's existence, and the stress on clear and distinct ideas. **Vico** thought it was all too reliant on mathematics, which was anyway constructed by Man. In place of the idea that the physical sciences could produce knowledge with geometric precision **Vico** put the principle of **'Verum factum'** or **'Truth is Deed'**: *We can only know for certain that which we have made or created.*

From this idea **Vico** developed his views on historical understanding. (Historical studies were very backward at the time — the sciences were making all the running).
He argued that since society, or the "world of nations" had been made by man, it could only be understood in terms of men and their behaviour. He was radical in rejecting a fixed idea of man's nature, and looking at development and change in society as a whole. He argued that the various aspects of a society formed a coherent, inter-related pattern.
Vico also stressed the importance of looking at language, myth, law and ritual in the workings of a society — an idea which is currently commonplace, but unheard of in his day. He was naturally mostly ignored in his lifetime, and for a century afterwards, while Continental Rationalism ruled the roost.
All of these ideas about history were being put into practice back in England where, probably for the first and last time, revolutions and counter-revolutions were going on. Roundheads and longhairs got the chop as radicals were replaced by second-hand kings.

Winstanley

Overton

Rainsborough

Lilburne

Meanwhile back in England ...

Things were beginning to happen. In fact three major things:

- **THE ENGLISH CIVIL WAR** The first revolution in which a class, the bourgeoisie, overthrew a monarchy and a feudal order
- **EMPIRICISM** Starting from **Hobbes'** nominalist theory of language — words have no corresponding reality in or out of the mind, being mere words — this was a reaction to continental rationalism and asserted that

  KNOWLEDGE IS BASED ON EXPERIENCE

  (like all other theories, this is not as simple as it sounds)
- **LIBERALISM & DEMOCRACY** These ideas were associated with the rising middle-classes of England and Holland, who rejected everything mediaeval. Religious toleration, democratic freedoms, the rights of property and a regard for commerce and industry were central, as were a belief in the equality of men and the importance of education.

In the figure of

John Locke
(1632 - 1704)

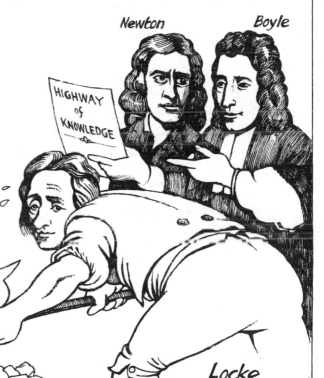

Newton   Boyle

HIGHWAY OF KNOWLEDGE

We can see some of the inter-connections. He was a philosopher, a political theorist, and the embodiment of the spirit of the bourgeois democratic revolution of 1688 in which a constitutional monarch replaced the short-lived Commonwealth.

Unlike the creators of rationalist systems, LOCKE had a more modest objective.

··TO BE EMPLOYED AS AN UNDER-LABOURER IN CLEARING THE GROUND A LITTLE, AND REMOVING SOME OF THE RUBBISH THAT LIES IN THE WAY OF KNOWLEDGE

metaphysical rubbish

First, **Locke's** theory of knowledge. We'll come back to his political theories.

Locke

Born to a Somerset family of the minor gentry who supported the Parliamentary cause in the Civil War, he studied medicine & chemistry at Oxford. After reading **Descartes** he became interested in philosophy and opposed to rationalism. He was 58 when his famous *"Essay Concerning Human Understanding"* was published.

Locke had a distaste for metaphysics. He wrote to a friend about **Leibniz:**
"You and I have had enough of this kind of fiddling".
He disagreed with **Plato's** theory of universals, and denied *any* innate ideas
"The mind is furnished with ideas by experience alone"

For **Locke,** the mind of the new-born child is like a blank sheet of paper.

All ideas are acquired from experience, and are of two kinds:

1 **Ideas of SENSATION** — seeing, hearing etc. (The input from the senses)

2 **Ideas of REFLECTION** — thinking, believing etc. (The different operations of the mind)

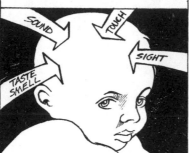

The first ideas are **SIMPLE** ones of sensation, then of reflection, where the mind is essentially *passive*. Later, the mind in an *active* way forms **COMPLEX** ideas by combining, or companing, or abstracting from simple ideas.

Thus, even the imaginary idea of a unicorn is really made up from simple ideas coming from sense-experience

 HORSE + HORN  = UNICORN

Locke poses a little riddle which clarifies his theory:

A man, blind from birth, can distinguish a sphere & cube by touch....

Suddenly given sight, can he tell them apart without touching?

BUT WHAT'S THE RELATIONSHIP BETWEEN THE IDEA & THE OBJECT ITSELF?

OBJECTS HAVE **QUALITIES** WHICH PRODUCE AN IDEA IN THE MIND

ROCK-LIKE QUALITIES

BEAM ME UP SCOTTIE

Locke said there were **PRIMARY** & **SECONDARY** QUALITIES. Primary qualities "really do exist in the bodies themselves." Secondary qualities produce ideas in the mind which aren't in the object.

> LET ME SEE — SO A **PRIMARY** QUALITY OF A NUT IS ITS **HARDNESS**, BUT ITS COLOUR IS A **SECONDARY** QUALITY?

This isn't as nutty as it sounds: **Locke** was trying to distinguish between **APPEARANCE** & **REALITY**.

Locke's theory, deriving initialy from Newtonian physics, was to prove tremendously influential. He thought he had explained the origin of all our ideas, and how we come to know the world out there. But many disagreed with him.

His first serious critic was

George **Berkeley**
(1685 – 1753)

> YOU SAY THAT ALL OUR KNOWLEDGE COMES FROM SENSATION OR REFLECTION?

> AND YOU SAY THIS ROCK & NUT ACT ON OUR MINDS TO PRODUCE 'IDEAS'?

> WELL, IF YOU WERE CONSISTENT, YOU WOULD HAVE TO ADMIT THAT **ALL** WE HAVE IS YOUR 'IDEAS', AND THAT WE CAN'T KNOW ANYTHING ABOUT THE ROCK ITSELF OR THE NUT ITSELF

> IN SHORT, YOUR THEORY ABOUT 'QUALITIES' IS TOTALLY **ROCKY**, NOT TO SAY **NUTS**

An outstandingly lucid thinker and limpid writer, the Anglo-Irish **Berkeley** was both don and cleric, ending his days as Bishop of Cloyne. His attempt to win support for a missionary college in Bermuda failed, as did his project to convince the world of the miraculous medicinal properties of tar-water.

Spirit of John Locke

83

Locke said **abstract ideas** were formed by jumping from a series of particular ideas:

PARTICULAR TRIANGLES

ABSTRACT IDEA OF A TRIANGLE

Berkeley insisted that all such 'abstract ideas' are really only
              particular ideas ..

Dr Samuel Johnson's response was crude:

But what causes the pain in Johnson's toe?

The rock?
The 'idea' of the rock
God?
Terminal gout?

84

David Hume
(1711 – 1776)

was the most important and influential of the British empiricists both because he developed empiricism to its logical conclusion and more or less destroyed it by doing so. Born in Edinburgh of Scottish parents he became a notable literary figure and published a major **History of England**. He was seen as an atheist, a sceptic and the leader of the Scottish Enlightenment. His most important philosophical work **A Treatise of Human Nature** was published when he was only 28 and "it fell dead-born from the press". Amongst the aims of the **Treatise** were to establish, *"what objects our understandings were, or were not fitted to deal with"*, and a science of man which would introduce the experimental method of reasoning into moral subjects.

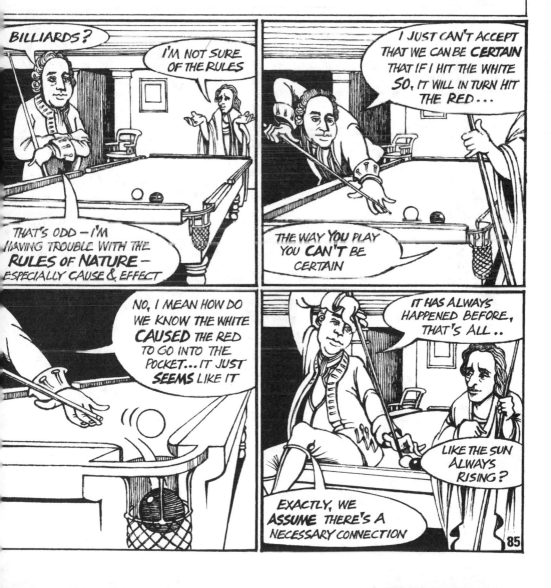

Hume had set out to create the foundations of a genuinely empirical science of human nature and ended up undermining them.

Political Philosophy

The beheading of Charles I and the creation of parliamentary democracy in 17th century England were the most obvious signs of political change, and not unnaturally there was a revival of political philosophy too. This revival was underpinned by the advances in science, the growth of religious toleration and the rise of philosophical liberalism.

From **Plato**'s *"Republic"* onwards philosophers had been faced with the political implications of their thought, but many had avoided the question.

The Greeks had tended to think of man as a communal being within the state, mediaeval thinkers considered the role of the state within the Christian synthesis, whereas modern political philosophy looked at **the individual and the state**.

Machiavelli had attempted a detached political science in the 16th century, but it was **HOBBES** who first expressed the characteristic problems of modern political philosophy.

Hobbes, you will remember, was a determinist materialist who tried to found a mechanical science of man, in which 'civil philosophy' would be the political equivalent of Galileo's natural science. Opposed to the English Revolution, and in favour of a strong monarch, **Hobbes** set out his political philosophy in

"Leviathan"

MAN IS A WOLF TO MAN

In the STATE of NATURE man relentlessly pursues survival at the expense of others, in a war of all against all

Good & evil are only what men make them – what is important is Man's fundamental selfishness. But men are also rational. To aid survival, they logically follow the 'natural law': "SEEK PEACE & FOLLOW IT"

They recognise that the war of all against all is only anarchy, & renounce some of their rights by entering into a SOCIAL CONTRACT

This creates an artificial man, a commonwealth in which the sovereign is the sum of the individuals

In this state Hobbes saw the ruler as absolute, men having no right to rebel since this would break the SOCIAL CONTRACT and be illogical.

As these deductions are meant to be scientific Hobbes says to break any law is wrong and that therefore there cannot be an unjust law — possibly a bad one — but not unjust.

Hobbes wasn't very interested in individual liberty but this was the major interest of

John Locke

His two "Treatises on Government" were published in 1689 and 1690, the years after the Glorious Revolution in England which gave the bourgeoisie parliamentary power within a constitutional monarchy.

YOU COULD ADD THAT HE WAS THE FATHER OF LIBERALISM, THE EPITOME OF EMPIRICISM'S REASONABLENESS & THE SPIRITUAL GUIDE OF THE AMERICAN CONSTITUTION

Thomas Jefferson

Governments are instituted among Men, deriving their just powers from the consent of the governed

AND THAT HIS INFLUENCE ON THE ENLIGHTENMENT WAS ENORMOUS...

D'Alembert

L'Encyclopédie

In his first **Treatise** Locke argued that there was no divine right for monarchs to rule, since God didn't put some men above others. In his second **Treatise** he attacks Hobbes and puts forward a liberal interpretation of the State of Nature. *"Man is free and in this condition all men are equal"*.

According to **Locke** men knew moral law even in the State of Nature:

"Reason, which is that law, teaches all mankind who will but consult it, that, being all equal and independent, no one ought to harm another in his life, health, liberty or profession."

WHAT ABOUT SLAVERY?

IT'S EXCUSED AS THE OUTCOME OF A "JUST WAR"!

As secretary of the Board of Trade & Plantations, Locke profited from slavery...

ARE YOU A FREE INDIVIDUAL, A SLAVE, OR A NOBLE SAVAGE?

For Locke & Hobbes, the starting point was the free individual. A popular fiction of the time was 'Robinson Crusoe!'

Being a good bourgeois, **Locke** thought the right of private property was particularly implied by natural law. He argued that the justification of private ownership lay in labour, and was therefore natural.

This important idea was based on the notion that since a man's labour was his own, anything he transformed by his labour should become, and remain, his as well. Property gave a man rights too, such as the right to kill anyone who tried to nick his property.

Indeed property, for **Locke**, is the main reason men leave the state of nature and set up civil government.

TO EXPLAIN HOW **LABOUR** CONFERS RIGHTS, **LOCKE** GIVES THE EXAMPLE :

"*Thus the Grass my horse has bit: the Turfs my servant has cut become my* **Property**. *The labour that was mine has fixed my property in them*"

WHAT ABOUT **MY** LABOUR ?

ALL MINE

THE GREAT & CHIEF END OF MEN UNITING INTO COMMONWEALTHS & PUTTING THEMSELVES UNDER GOVERNMENT IS THE PRESERVATION OF THEIR PROPERTY

For **Locke** the point of having a king, laws and a civil society under a social contract is so that men can enjoy their **INALIENABLE RIGHTS**, which are ordained by God.

They are :

1 The **Right to Life**
  2 The **Right to Liberty**
    3 The **Right to Property**

4 The **Right to Rebel** against unjust rulers & laws

DO **WE** HAVE ANY RIGHTS ?

89

The **poor** do not share in Locke's democratic rights. Neither do **women** ..

ISN'T IT TIME FOR A VINDICATION OF THE **RIGHTS** OF WOMEN?

The most radical part of Locke's political theory was that of **CHECKS and BALANCES** within the state. He was talking about Kings and Parliaments, which he called the executive and legislative powers respectively. Instead of absolute monarchy he said there should be a **separation** of power and the legislative should be supreme. This parliament ought to be removable by the people and if the executive — King, President — refuses to listen to or call such a parliament the executive could be removed by force. Clearly this was a product of the experience of the English civil war. "**Force**, Locke said, *is to be opposed to nothing but unjust and unlawful force*." It is of course difficult to decide when force is "unjust and unlawful" and it is usually force that decides the question.

It was force that did just that in the American Revolution, upon whose founding fathers Locke had a clear influence. The American Declaration of Independence (1776) and the American Constitution embody both the idea of rights and of separation of the parts of Government. **Baron Montesquieu**, the French political theorist, transmitted Locke's ideas to the American Revolution and added the separation of the judiciary. In the American Constitution the President, the Congress and the judiciary are to this day separate.

Locke's reasonable presentation of the liberal compromise of bourgeois England was set however to produce radical ferment throughout a Europe of absolutist monarchies.

The Age of Reason

England settled down after 1688 and Berkeley & Hume weren't very interested in political philosophy. Because of the reputation of Newtonian science and Locke's liberalism all progressives in 18th century Europe looked to England. The 18th C. has generally been called the age of Enlightenment, or just The **Enlightenment** because of the spread of rational, progressive, liberal and scientific ideas. Everyone seemed to think that if only the right sorts of answers to all sorts of problems could be discovered then mankind could take a leap forward into a new scientific age. Everyone thought philosophy would become a sort of natural science of the soul in which objective answers to all the complicated problems of knowledge would just pop out when you looked carefully at them. It was a hopeful, noble and inspiring age but as somebody said 'things fall apart'.

France was still a divine monarchy in which an antiquated and corrupt system of government was increasingly disliked by almost everyone, but particularly the intellectuals.

The nobility in the 18th century tried to seize power for themselves whereas the middle-class produced a radical intelligentsia who created the conditions for the French Revolution of 1789. On the surface Church and State seemed strong but below the intellectuals were writing, thinking and reflecting on the corruptness of absolutism.

Power must limit power

Voltaire (1694-1778)

n the other hand was a radical, a liberal and trongly anti-Christian, as were most of the hilosophes. From 1726–9 **Voltaire** was in England nd became an exponent of the philosophy and olitics of Locke. His "*Letters concerning the nglish Nation*" were called "the first bomb hurled gainst the Old Regime", this being a reflection of heir impact in disseminating the radical liberal deas of English political philosophy.

oltaire single-handedly set out to enlighten rance and he wrote poems, plays, histories, eatises, translations and novels which add up to ome 70 volumes. His main philosophical ontribution was in the realm of natural religion. y this Voltaire meant that nature is the work of God nd that man was the product of nature, not simply f God. Voltaire was attempting to set man free from rthodox Christian views.

Most of all Voltaire wanted philosophy to be useful, o change the way people behaved. In "*The gnorant Philosopher*" he argued that philosophy was useless if "no philosopher has had any nfluence even on the morals of the street where he ved."

he problem of nature and evil was one that also xercised Voltaire's mind in his fight against rthodoxy. Against **Leibniz** and the other ptimists' and against those who, like **Pascal**, rgued a pessimistic theology of man's depravity, oltaire tried to find a middle course in which man, hrough reason, found moral virtue. Voltaire clearly rought out the moral dilemma of the new hilosophy and its conception of nature:

Baron Montesquieu (1689-1755)

was the first of the so-called philosophes (Enlightenment thinkers) to articulate this criticism in his "*Persian Letters*" (1721) and then in his most famous work "*The Spirit of the Laws*" (1748). An aristocrat himself he wanted to see a constitutional monarchy like that of England and a politically progressive and responsible nobility. Paradoxically his critical work initiated the movement that would destroy the possibility of both in France.

The spirit of the laws was written after 14 years study of political history and philosophy, particularly that of Locke. In it Montesquieu looked for the "nature and principle" that underlay different kinds of laws. He classified forms of government according to their "animating principle". He argued that:

> Virtue was the principle of a Republic
> Honour that of a monarchy
> Fear of a despotism.

In examining the interconnections between the various aspects of a society and its laws Montesquieu initiated the study of the bonds between political patterns and social forms which was to lead to what we now call the political and social sciences.

The Lisbon Earthquake of 1747

IF NATURE IS **GOOD**, THEN THERE IS NO **EVIL**, IF THERE IS **EVIL**, THEN NATURE CANNOT IN ITSELF BE **GOOD**

The Enlightenment was to have quite a few problems with this one.

Leading member of economists known as the **Physiocrats**. A materialist, argued in *"The Economic Table"* wealth came from the land, and that the principle of *"laissez-faire"* best helped the general good.

Naturalist. Opposed to rigid classification of **Linnaeus**. Argued for Great Chain of Being:
Nature as an inter-connected web.

Empirical scientist. Co-editor of *Encyclopédia*, aimed at secularisation of knowledge based on belief in science, progress and the perfectability of man:
"To change the common way of thinking."

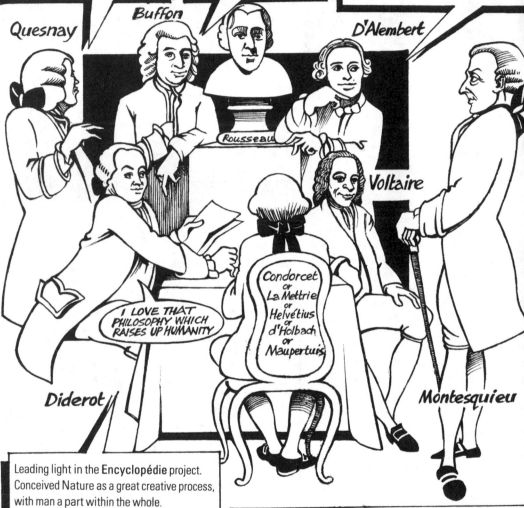

Quesnay

Buffon

Rousseau

D'Alembert

Voltaire

I LOVE THAT PHILOSOPHY WHICH RAISES UP HUMANITY

Condorcet or La Mettrie or Helvétius or d'Holbach or Maupertuis

Diderot

Montesquieu

Leading light in the **Encyclopédie** project. Conceived Nature as a great creative process, with man a part within the whole. Stressed the relativity of culture, and the necessity for change.
Bohemian, occasionally imprisoned, he represented the radical spirit of
"A new world is born".

In *"Rameau's Nephew"* attacked bourgeois conformism.

SOME ESSENTIAL IDEAS of the ENLIGHTENMENT
1. *Man is not innately depraved.*
2. *The aim of life is life itself, not the after-life.*
3. *The essential condition for the good life on earth is freeing men's minds from ignorance and superstition.*
4. *Man, free of ignorance and of the arbitrary powers of the state, is capable of progress and perfection.*
5. *Everything is inter-connected, and forms part of the grand scheme of a benevolent Providence.*

*After **Locke** and **Hume** English philosophy seemed to settle down and play a less important role in the Enlightenment. Whilst France underwent intellectual and eventually political upheaval the English bourgeoisie concentrated on trade, wealth and agriculture.*

Edmund Burke
(1729 - 97)

was the very model of an 18th century philosopher. A statesman, an essayist and originally a supporter of liberal ideas he was in favour of American independence but recoiled from the mass democracy of the French Revolution and wrote his famous *"Reflections on the Revolution in France"*, which has become a conservative textbook on the dangers of radicalism. He points to the dangers of the "new dealers" in France and to their despotic tendencies which he contrasts with the good sense and liberalism of England, a theme which is often repeated in Engish politics. **Burke** also wrote a philosophical treatise on the *"Origins of our ideas of the Sublime and the Beautiful"*, in which he puts forward a very interesting argument that it is obscurity and suggestiveness rather than clarity that captures the imagination. This argument could be applied to philosophy rather than beauty.

LEARNING WILL BE CAST INTO THE MIRE & TRODDEN DOWN UNDER THE HOOFS OF A SWINISH MULTITUDE

A staunch political opponent of Burke's conservatism was

Tom Paine
(1737-1809)

whose *"The Rights of Man"* was a counterblast to the former's conservatism, a defence of democracy and a statement of republican principles. **Paine** achieved fame when he published *"Common Sense"* in which he argued for American Independence and for governments to be made strictly accountable to the people, to be tolerated only if they achieved for them "Life, liberty and the pursuit of happiness". Any government who didn't achieve this should be thrown out according to **Paine**, and by force if necessary. **Paine** also fought for the American Revolution, published pamphlets in its support and helped to formulate both the Declaration of Independence and the Declaration of the Rights of Man. His clear and logical defence of the French Revolution made him very popular in certain quarters in England and deeply unpopular in others. **Paine** attacked Christianity in his *"The Age of Reason"* but from the point of view of natural religion, or Deism, rather than that of atheism. **Paine** was what we might call a practical philosopher who acted upon what he thought and thereby influenced the world.

Someone who rarely gets mentioned either in history or philosophy is

Mary Wollstonecraft
(1759–1797)

HYENA!
SERPENT.

This may be because what she had to say wasn't quite what even the enlightened, never mind the reactionary, intellectuals of her day wanted to hear. Her *"Vindication of the Rights of Woman"* can be seen as the feminist declaration of independence to mirror that of the American and *Paine's "Rights of Man"*.

What **Wollstonecraft** did was to take the liberal doctrine of inalienable human rights and apply them to women. She argued **"Mind has no sex"** and therefore rights are not determined by gender. This was an important and radical extension of liberal ideas, mostly ignored by other philosophers and critics.

The reaction to her writing was extraordinary, she was called a "philosophizing serpent", a "hyena in petticoats" and one of the "impious amazons of Republican France". Clearly there were still limits to the love of wisdom and the search for truth.

Wollstonecraft argued for women's complete personal and economic independence and against most of the images of women that other philosophers, including **Rousseau** perpetrated.

Mary also travelled to France and wrote *"A Vindication of the Rights of Men"* which defended the civil and religious liberties of the French Revolution. She died in childbirth at the age of 38.

A solid supporter of the English bourgeoisie and its new found power, which had been won through economic progress, was

Adam Smith
(1723–1790)

> THE STUDY OF A MAN'S OWN ADVANTAGE **NECESSARILY** LEADS HIM TO PREFER WHAT IS MOST ADVANTAGEOUS TO SOCIETY

He studied moral philosophy in Glasgow and was part of the Scottish 'Enlightenment' which is always seen as English. His *"Theory of the Moral Sentiments"* is practically forgotten but his *"Wealth of Nations"* definitely isn't. **Hume** read it on his death-bed and immediately recognised its importance. **Smith** is the classic exponent of the idea of individualism within society, but gave it an economic twist. According to **Adam Smith** society is a commercial enterprise in which morality is derived from the market-place.

"Economic freedom is the obvious & simple system of natural liberty."

Smith was saying that the unintended consequences of allowing everyone free economic rein would be the greater welfare of all, even though the intended result was selfish accumulation. Not surprisingly the bourgeoisie loved this idea that the way to be moral was to be greedy. This explains why **Smith's** ideas are still popular with lots of people, particularly those in business.

The originator of the "Romantic" sensibility, whose influence spread throughout Europe in the late 18th and 19th centuries was

Jean-Jacques Rousseau
(1712 - 78)

He started out as a contributor to the Encyclopaedia but then moved away from the philosophies to argue for **feeling** rather than **reason** as the basis for an approach to theology and politics.

This was a revolutionary and original shift that undermined the intellectualist and determinist approach of the Enlightenment.

Rousseau was in many ways like his ideas: original, difficult, brilliant and sometimes completely wrong. He was also cantankerous, passionate, poetic and occasionally paranoid. Unlike some philosophers, however, he was never dull....

> I COULD NOT DISSEMBLE FROM MYSELF THAT THE HOLY DEED I WAS ABOUT TO DO WAS AT BOTTOM THE ACT OF A BANDIT

Born of fairly humble parents in Calvinist Geneva, **Rousseau** ran away from home when he was sixteen, and had himself converted to Catholicism. He hiked around Europe on foot, became a lackey to a Madame de Vercelli, lived with a Madame de Warens, then masqueraded as a Scottish Jacobite and became secretary to the French ambassador in Venice in 1743. In 1745 he met Thérèse de Vasseur, a servant girl at his Paris hotel, and they lived together until his death. Thérèse was by all accounts, neither literate, beautiful, faithful nor very sober. Rousseau had five children by her, all of whom he took off to the Foundling Hospital. This extraordinary behaviour was very unromantic, but Rousseau was particularly good at living with contradictions, which his autobiography, *"Confessions"*, makes abundantly clear. In it he presented himself as the model of an estranged 'modern man', cut off from his true nature.

FOUNDLING HOSPITAL

ANOTHER ROUSSEAU BABY..

WELL, HE'S TOO BUSY WRITING ABOUT HOW TO RAISE CHILDREN...

Shelley

Lermontov

Byron

Pushkin

Keats

Leopardi

Wordsworth

95

His first great public success was his *"Discourse on the Arts & Sciences"*, in which he argued that the arts and sciences had *degraded* man, that science and virtue were incompatible, and that before the development of 'civilisation' men's morals were "rude but natural". This was the exact opposite of the philosophers' argument, and not surprisingly, they didn't like it. **Voltaire** in particular was very hostile.

In *"Emile"*, **Rousseau** outlined a libertarian method of education aimed at developing the child without destroying this "natural" state.

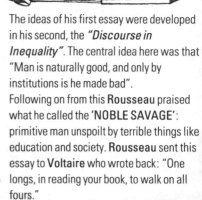

The ideas of his first essay were developed in his second, the *"Discourse in Inequality"*. The central idea here was that "Man is naturally good, and only by institutions is he made bad".

Following on from this **Rousseau** praised what he called the '**NOBLE SAVAGE**': primitive man unspoilt by terrible things like education and society. **Rousseau** sent this essay to **Voltaire** who wrote back: "One longs, in reading your book, to walk on all fours."

Actually, **Rousseau** meant that primitive man seemed to live in organic unity with himself, in harmony, whereas modern man was cut off from himself. Everyone took him just to be saying: 'Act like primitives'.

His view of religion, that feeling, emotion and awe were a kind of proof of God, also became influential, indeed so completely that one forgets **Rousseau** dreamt it up. Putting the heart before reason, poetry before science, stressing feeling, emotion and imagination, was central to Romanticism.

Back to Nature

For Voltaire, in his satire *"L'Ingénu"* the **NOBLE SAVAGE** was a Huron Indian...

For Montesquieu, it was the Englishman!

Rousseau's political theory was also extremely important, not least in its influence on the **French Revolution**. In his *"Social Contract"* he argued for the extension of democracy to all, and for 'direct democracy' rather than 'elective aristocracy', which is what he called elected representatives.

"Man is born free and everywhere he is in chains"

Rousseau saw primitive man locked up again in society through the social contract. He wanted to resolve this contradiction.

HOW DO YOU WORK OUT A PACT THAT COMBINES THE BEST OF THE NECESSARY EVIL OF SOCIETY & OF THE STATE OF NATURE?

THROUGH THE **GENERAL WILL**

WHAT'S THAT?

NOT JUST THE WILL OF ALL, BUT MORE AN ABSTRACT EXPRESSION OF WHAT IS BEST FOR ALL

LIKE HOBBES' **LEVIATHAN**?

YES, BUT EACH INDIVIDUAL **VOLUNTARILY** SUBJUGATES HIMSELF TO THE COLLECTIVE GENERAL WILL... ..WHICH BECOMES THE SOLE SOURCE OF SOVEREIGNTY

WHAT ABOUT PARTICIPATORY DEMOCRACY? DISAGREEMENTS ARISING FROM INDIVIDUAL OPINIONS CANCEL EACH OTHER OUT: THE GENERAL WILL EMERGES

SOUNDS A BIT **ROMANTIC** BUT IN THIS WAY THE INDIVIDUAL DEVELOPS WITHIN A FRAMEWORK OF SOCIAL EQUALITY, THROUGH THE LAW

According to **Rousseau** man can be *forced* to be free within the law. The general will only considers the common interest, which is liberty & equality. The **'Sovereign'** expresses the general will in action, and 'by virtue of what it is', is always right.

Rousseau's political theory marked a major turning-point in the Enlightenment, giving expression to an all-pervasive sense of disillusionment that found its complete expression in the French Revolution.

The aristocracy adopted **Rousseau**'s primitivism, playing at "back to nature", which elevated the country life and further alienated the upper classes from the average Frenchman. The bourgeoisie aped the aristocracy, but the masses took to **Rousseau**'s ideas of total participatory democracy.

Indeed the *"Social Contract"* became the bible of many of the leaders of the Revolution, particularly the Jacobins.

Robespierre

APPARENTLY, IT'S THE GENERAL WILL

Rousseau is still blamed by some for the bloody bits of the Revolution. His ideas were more complex than that; at base he expressed the sense of the loss of nature which all Romantics, including Goethe and Lessing, were to embrace.

The German ENLIGHTENMENT

In many ways the progressive thought of the Enlightenment was bound up with the economic and political success of the new bourgeoisie. It is therefore not surprising that the still feudalistic principalities of Germany produced neither a strong middle-class nor a body of radical thought comparable to England or France. Philosophy was not dead, however, it just took more introspective forms.

Leibniz was still influential through his follower

Christian Wolff (1659–1754)

A professor of philosophy, he had a highly systematic approach which provided German philosophy with a language, a programme and methods which survived for a long time. He wrote a lot, of which his work on Leibniz' *Philosophia Prima Sive Ontologia* is the most important.

He rejected empiricism and argued that philosophy was the precise delineation of concepts and essences, not of experience. Like **Kant**, who was to call him an "excellent analyst", **Wolff** seemed to be trying to reconcile rationalism and the naturalism of Enlightenment thought.

Because of the servile role the intelligentsia played within an economically and socially backward nation like Germany, where the nobility still ran the show, it is not entirely surprising that inward looking philosophical ideas developed. There was a sharp opposition between thought and social reality and between an idealised past and a dismal present. The roots of Romanticism lay in these contradictions. Romantic thought, which gave priority to feeling and imagination, was opposed to both rationalism and empiricism and argued for a knowledge of the self through art and literature as well as through philosophy. The romantic reaction to Enlightenment thought often incorporated aspects of the Enlightenment however, and developed them in original ways.

Gotthold Lessing (1729–81)

historian, dramatist, and theologian exemplified these contradictory elements. He was in the mould of the English and French free thinkers, but said that the rational intellect of **Locke** and **Newton** could not penetrate to the true heart of reality. In his *Laöcoon* he argued for an art founded on the free expression of feeling. He tried to put this into practice through drama, by founding a reformed theatre that could enlighten the German people. He wanted to write radical middle-class plays that would attack the nobility and their aping of French manners and customs. His tragedies tended to turn out as melodramas however.

His historical views were important too as he began a critique of religion that would provide the fundamental ideas for **Hegel**'s philosophy of religion. He believed in an evolutionary view of religion in which man grew up, as it were, and passed out of the phase in which religion was necessary.

Herder

(1774-1803) also reflected the confused impulses of German thought, he held to the idea of progress but could only express it in a mystical, romantic idea of the nation. Since political and social conditions in Germany precluded reform **Herder** suggested that a cultural and spiritual awakening was needed. He saw the nation not as a political entity but as a **Volk** with a common cultural heritage. This mystical nationalist force would express itself through metamorphosis, in a natural way, since culture was seen as a natural attribute. These romantic notions were to reappear in much uglier forms under fascism. His ideas were set out in *"Philosophy of the History of Man"*

J.W. van Goethe
(1749-1832)

As a young man **Goethe** was a prime mover in the anarchic romanticism of the **Sturm und Drang** (Storm & Stress) movement. But his great poem *"Faust"*, sixty years in the writing, went far beyond the romantic reaction, ending in the spiritual and material upheavals of the industrial revolution. Faust sells his soul to the Devil in the end not for money, sex or fame but for the right to control Nature, to transform the mediaeval world through massive organised labour.

Faust becomes the first **developer** — the archetypal modern entrepreneur.

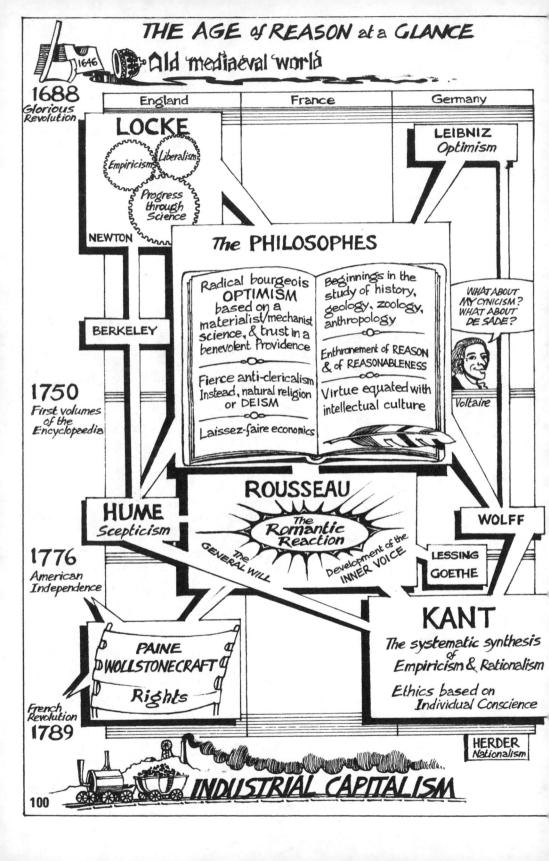

We left empiricism under the table, Hume having demolished its claims to knowledge, and rationalism out of the window with Leibniz's monads. Then the Enlightenment thought it had sorted everything out and Rousseau and the romantic reaction threw reason into disarray. Fortunately **Immanuel Kant** came along and provided a grand synthesis, a new direction and a whole new mode of philosophy. No-one realised it at the time however.

(God said that if Kant hadn't existed someone would have had to invent him.)

Immanuel Kant (1724 - 1804)

Kant was born in Königsberg in 1724 where he spent his whole life, becoming a professor at the university and dying there in 1804.

He was a person of incredibly regular habits, and almost as regular a producer of papers and books. People in Königsberg used to set their watches by him as he went on his daily walk. His publications however were interrupted between 1770-81 when he produced nothing at all. This was probably because he was thinking extremely hard about his great work the *Critique of Pure Reason*, which is considered to make Kant the *"greatest of modern philosophers"*. Unlike Rousseau absolutely nothing at all occurred in Kant's life that could be described as interesting, he didn't even get married, have a serious illness or keep a pet. His only deviation seems to have been when he first read Rousseau's *Emile*, he stayed in for several days to re-read it and people all over Königsberg were late for things.

The Day Kant read "Emile"

YOU'RE LATE!

I'M LATE!

WE'RE LATE!

THEY'RE LATE

In philosophy Kant started off being influenced by Wolff's version of Leibniz, a highly systematic rationalism that held sway in German universities. Reading Hume awakened him from his dogmatic slumbers and he was never the same again. His early work was scientific and naturalist, including his *Dissertation on Fire, On Earthquakes and Winds* and his *General History of Nature and Theory of the Heavens*. After his decade of silence came the three great critiques *Pure Reason, Critique of Practical Reason* and in 1790 the *Critique of Judgement*.

Dogmatic Slumbers

HUME

WOLFF

His pre-critical period (before 1781) saw him writing on many things; on Leibniz, God, the beautiful and the sublime, on space and particularly on metaphysics. During this period Kant broke away from Wolff's ideas and was influenced by Enlightenment ideas, by empiricism and importantly by Newton's scientific ideas. He was worried by rationalism's inability to demonstrate existence, like Descartes who thought he had. He was also worried by empiricism's inability to demonstrate how experience became knowledge. There didn't seem to be a solid basis for philosophy and this is what he wanted to establish.

Even more precisely he posed the question in his critical works

Can metaphysics exist as a science?

Metaphysics you will remember was the attempt to understand the whole world, the universe in its totality, to go beyond science and its separate facts and construct explanations. Lots of people, like Hume argued that metaphysics is an impossibility.

To put that another way Kant thought science was doing marvellous things but that this left him with real problems about philosophy, which didn't seen to produce much except dead ends like metaphysics or empiricism. Nothing that could be seen as hard evidence anyway.

What Kant meant was that the problem of how scientists knew things turned out to be very similar to the problem of how metaphysicians knew things about abstract ideas like freedom or morality. In science and metaphysics he said that human kind starts off with data which is worked on and gives rise to a judgement, the process being similar.

THE GENUINE METHOD OF METAPHYSICS IS FUNDAMENTALLY THAT WHICH NEWTON BROUGHT TO SCIENCE & WHICH WAS THERE SO FRUITFUL.

So KANT set out,

in his "CRITIQUE OF PURE REASON," to discover the true capacities of thought

But first a PHILOSOPHICAL HEALTH WARNING from the horse's mouth

IT'S A BIT HARD, IMMANUEL

WORSE — IT'S DRY, OBSCURE, CONTRARY TO ALL ORDINARY IDEAS, & ON TOP OF THAT, PROLIX

And second, some technical terms

Kant used the traditional distinction between **ANALYTIC** & **SYNTHETIC** propositions.
Analytic propositions only eludicate words — e.g. Billiard balls are spherical.
Synthetic propositions go beyond this — e.g.

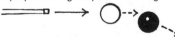

The white billiard ball struck so will cause black ball to go in the direction indicated

Kant added two other terms.
A PRIORI knowledge he defined as that coming purely from reasoning, independent of experience,
&**A POSTERIORI** knowledge as that coming from experience.

EMPIRICISM

All knowledge comes from experience

There are no innate ideas

Has problems proving the logical necessity of experiential laws

Synthetic propositions
A posteriori knowledge

RATIONALISM

Knowledge comes from logical, rational deduction

Innate ideas form the only secure basis for knowledge

Has problems linking its logical certainty with reality

Analytic propositions
A priori knowledge

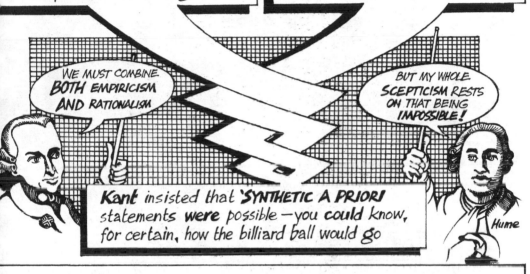

WE MUST COMBINE **BOTH** EMPIRICISM **AND** RATIONALISM

BUT MY WHOLE **SCEPTICISM RESTS** ON THAT BEING **IMPOSSIBLE!**

Kant insisted that '**SYNTHETIC A PRIORI** statements **were** possible — you **could** know, for certain, how the billiard ball would go

Hume

For **Kant**, knowledge came from a **synthesis** of experience and concepts: without the senses we should not become aware of any object, but without understanding we should form no conception of it.
The process of gaining knowledge was a unified one involving perception, imagination and understanding: sensibility and understanding were in inter-action.

PURE THOUGHT
SENSE EXPERIENCE

Kant went on to explain exactly how he thought the process worked.
First, he said **SPACE AND TIME** were given to everyone as a **priori pure intuitions**. They were absolute — independent of, and preceding sense impressions.
Secondly, he proposed **CATEGORIES of THOUGHT** which structured the way we grasp reality.
These were a sort of **basic conceptual apparatus** for making sense of the world.

NEW!
WITH ADDED
CATEGORIES

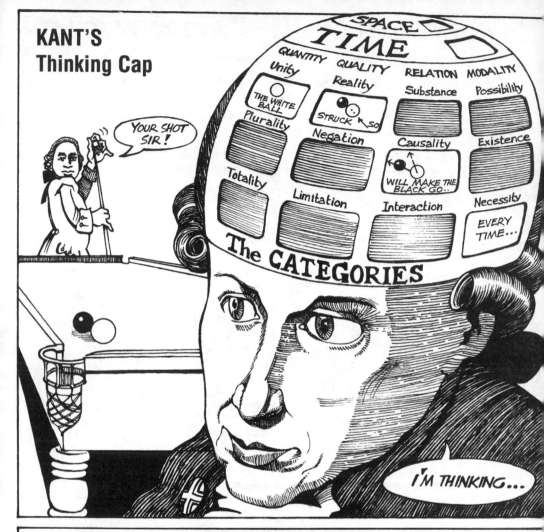

KANT'S Thinking Cap

SPACE
TIME

QUANTITY QUALITY RELATION MODALITY

Unity — Reality — Substance — Possibility

THE WHITE BALL

STRUCK SO

Plurality — Negation — Causality — Existence

WILL MAKE THE BLACK GO...

Totality — Limitation — Interaction — Necessity

EVERY TIME...

The CATEGORIES

YOUR SHOT SIR!

I'M THINKING...

The LIMITS of KNOWLEDGE

Having dealt with **Hume**'s billiard ball, let's go back to **Berkeley**'s rock.

Kant had no problem with the rock's existence: "The mere consciousness of my own existence proves the existence of objects in space outside me."

But he set limits to knowledge. He distinguished between **Appearance** (the world of **phenomena**) and **Reality** (the world of **noumena**). He said that the mysterious substance of the rock, what he called the *ding-an-sich*, or *thing-in-itself* was *unknowable*.

The attempt to go beyond the phenomenal world, to apply concepts outside the limits set by their empirical application inevitably leads to paradoxes, fallacies and actual contradiction.

DING AN SICH

UNKNOWABLE

Kant argued that traditional metaphysical arguments about the soul, immortality, God and free will, all went beyond the limits of reason. Reason's legitimate employment is the practical sphere, in knowing the world.

104

> TWO THINGS FILL THE MIND WITH EVER NEW & INCREASING ADMIRATION AND AWE... THE STARRY HEAVENS ABOVE AND THE MORAL LAW WITHIN

Having solved, or claiming to have solved the fundamental problem of the foundations of knowledge, **Kant** set out in his second *"Critique"*, and in the *"Foundations of the Metaphysics of Morals"*, to establish reason's role in ethics.

> IS THERE A PURE PRACTICAL REASON — A **SCIENCE** OF ETHICS?

> I BELIEVE THERE **IS** A PURE RATIONAL ELEMENT IN MORAL JUDGEMENTS...

> MORALITY COMES FROM REASON

> NOT FROM GOODNESS OF HEART, OR NATURE'S COMMANDS?

> NO — THE ONLY TRUE MORALITY IS THAT WHICH IS COMMANDED BY THE RIGOUR OF THOUGHT

> HOW DO WE **KNOW** THEN WHAT IS PROPER & WHAT ISN'T?

> I CANNOT TELL YOU IN EACH INSTANCE — ONLY THAT I HAVE DEDUCED A BASIC AXIOM FOR MORAL BEHAVIOUR..

— Kant called his axiom the **CATEGORICAL IMPERATIVE:**

ACT AS IF THE MAXIM FROM WHICH YOU ACT WERE TO BECOME THROUGH YOUR WILL A GENERAL LAW

For **Kant** this is a universal principle, binding on all men. In particular, **Kant** thought any action performed from self-interest could not be virtuous. Only an action which obeys the rational law of morality, which is also a duty, can be virtuous. The **CATEGORICAL IMPERATIVE** was, for **Kant**, an iron law. This was a major shift in thinking about morality. **Kant** gives no list of actions that are good or bad, only the internal rational principle on which we must always act.

Kant's rationalism led him to conclude that it was never right to tell a lie — even if someone wanted to murder your friend

" To tell a falsehood to a murderer who asked us whether our friend, of whom he was in pursuit, had taken refuge in our house, would be a crime "

105

This may be logically rigorous and philosophically coherent, but it sounds rather silly in a common-sense sort of way.

In his third *"Critique"* Kant tried to set out an objective basis for aesthetic judgement, to fit alongside the ethical theory.

Not surprisingly, he came up with a fairly rigid formula. He was sure that his thinking produced objective, universally valid ideas in morality, but felt he had to be a little more subjective about aesthetics.

He said, more or less, that although aesthetic judgements were *not* objectively valid, we should think of them *as if* they were.

To make it clearer, Kant used the phrase *"Purposiveness without purpose"* to describe what he looked for in art.

Kant also saw aesthetic judgement as a means to a greater end — the recognition of a purposiveness in Art and Nature, giving a kind of inspiration towards greater reason.

These ideas were very influential in future discussions of aesthetics.

AT THIS POINT WE INTRODUCE ONE OF THE UNWRITTEN LAWS OF PHILOSOPHY :

The greater the complexity or obscurity of a philosopher, the greater the likelihood of widely differing interpretations

HENCE THE NECESSITY FOR

THE CATEGORICAL INTERPRETATION

"Read any philosopher as if the interpretation you make were to become, through your interpretation, a general philosophical law"

The reason for putting this in is to draw attention to the fact that **Kant**, and **Hegel**, and others to come, are argued over by philosophers all the time. You have to agree on what they mean before you can disagree. This certainly happens with **Kant**, but that, as they say, is another story.

GERMAN IDEALISM

The school of idealism which grew up in Germany after Kant's death used a particular reading of his work and developed a speculative metaphysics, although Kant appeared to have denied such a possibility.

TO HAVE CHARACTER & BE GERMAN UNDOUBTEDLY MEAN ONE & THE SAME

Johann Gottlieb Fichte (1762-1814)

argued that the essence of **Kant**'s philosophy was that the subject, or **ego**, was the fundamental matter for enquiry. This version of **Kant**'s idea of practical knowledge, clearly took liberties with **Kant**.

Fichte ended up saying that the *"ding-an-sich"* didn't exist, and that the world was just "absolute ego', a sort of giant subject. This was taken up later by **Hegel** and German nationalists.

106

Friedrich von Schelling
(1775 – 1854)

ARCHITECTURE IS FROZEN MUSIC

was closely linked to the German romantics and tried to combine **Kant**'s critical philosophy with a broad account of the importance of art. In his *"System of Transcendental Idealism"* he had followed Fichte, but got fed up with it.

Friedrich von Schiller
(1759 – 1805)

SET THIS TO MUSIC & WE'VE GOT A HIT

developed **Kant's** ideas on art, arguing that art as a 'disinterested' activity, is central to both public and private life.
His ideas were part of the prevailing romantic attitude which saw art as indispensible.

Anne-Louise Germaine Necker, Baronne de Staël-Holstein, or Madame de Staël
(1766 – 1817)

was not in fact German, but wrote a famous book *"De L'Allemagne"*, in which she introduced the work of **Kant** and others to the French. Her clear exposition of **Kant**, **Fichte**, **Shelling** and **Schlegel** came as something of a revelation to the French, still mainly influenced by **Locke** and the Enlightenment.
Her other work, *"Literature considered in its connexions to social institutions"*, looked at the links between religion, law, morals and literature. It marked the beginning of what we now call the sociology of literature.

THE MORE I SEE OF MAN THE MORE I LIKE DOGS

G.W.F. Hegel
(1770–1831)

was the greatest of the German idealists, quite easily the most difficult to understand, and possibly the most outrageous in his claims to have understood the whole of history and philosophy.

He was a university lecturer and professor of philosophy for most of his life and, like **Kant**, did little else.

In old age he became a sort of semi-official Prussian philosopher and suggested that the Prussian state was probably the highest form of political organisation.

In his early days **Hegel** was something of a mystic, and some critics suggest he never overcame this trait. Of his many writings the most important are *"The Phenomenology of Mind"*, *"The Science of Logic"* and *"The Philosophy of Right"*.

The first two can probably claim to be the two most obscure books in the whole of philosophy, and have therefore produced the most interpretations.

*We can say that **Hegel** was influenced by three major movements, that his logic had a triadic structure, and his system a three-fold aspect:-*

INFLUENCES	Kant & post-Kantian idealism	Christianity	German Romanticism
LOGIC	Thesis	Antithesis	Synthesis
SYSTEM	Logic	Philosophy of Nature	Philosophy of Spirit

This is merely coincidence, since **Hegel** can be described as a **monist**, a believer in the one totality, the **ABSOLUTE SPIRIT**.

Hegel began by rejecting **Kant**'s thing-in-itself and he noumenal world. **Hegel** argued that **Kant**'s claim that something which existed (the thing-in-itself) was *unknowable*, was a clear contradiction, violating **Kant**'s own laws about the limits of knowledge.

The **Idealists**, and **Hegel**, put forward the opposite view that whatever *is*, is *knowable*. In **Hegel**'s famous dictum:

"The Real is Rational, & the Rational is Real"

IT'S EMPTY!

UNKNOWABLE

UNLIKE **KANT**, **HEGEL** SET NO LIMITS TO WHAT WAS KNOWABLE

Fundamental to **Hegel**'s thinking is the notion that *everything is inter-connected*. Whereas most philosophers from **Aristotle** on had argued that reality had to be separated into discrete parts — whether as facts, or objects, or monads — **Hegel** said *nothing was unrelated*.

For Hegel the Ulitmate Reality was the Absolute Idea, — *"the true is the whole"*. He equated Truth and System.

The individual piece only has meaning when it is seen as part of the whole jigsaw...

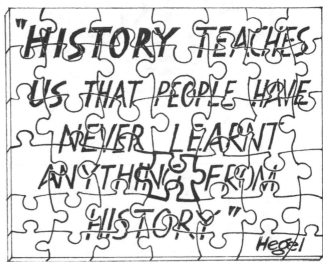

"HISTORY TEACHES US THAT PEOPLE HAVE NEVER LEARNT ANYTHING FROM HISTORY."

Hegel

WE HAVE TO SEE THE WORLD AS A DYNAMIC PROCESS — RATHER LIKE A **GIANT ORGANISM**

DON'T TELL ME — THE PROCESS IS THREE-FOLD

OF COURSE, & WHAT CONNECTS THE 3-FOLD REALITIES OF ABSOLUTE SPIRIT, NATURE, & MAN'S MIND IS A 3-FOLD MOVEMENT OF THOUGHT ITSELF — THE **DIALECTIC**

O.K — WHAT'S THAT ?

IT'S A PROCESS OF LOGIC BY WHICH WE DEDUCE FROM OUR EXPERIENCE THE CATEGORIES THAT LEAD TO THE ABSOLUTE

WOULD YOU EXPLAIN THAT — I'M JUST A BEGINNER

HAVE YOU GOT A SPARE TEN YEARS ?

The DIALECTIC

Here is how the system works. We start with a **THESIS** (a position put forward for argument). Opposed to this is a contradictory statement or **ANTITHESIS**. Out of their opposition comes a **SYNTHESIS** which embraces both.

But since the truth lies only in the whole system, this first **SYNTHESIS** is not yet the truth of the matter, but becomes a new thesis, with its corresponding antithesis and synthesis. The process continues ad infinitum until we reach the Absolute Idea.

O.K—I'LL GIVE YOU **THIS**..

..BUT WHAT'S THE **BIG IDEA** HERE ??

etc
etc

ULTIMATE SYNTHESIS
Absolute Idea

HEGEL
The Absolute Idea:
The idea, as unity of the Subjective and Objective Idea, is the notion of the Idea — a notion whose object (Gegenstand) is the Idea as such, and for which the objective (Objekt) is Idea — an Object which embraces all characteristics in its Unity.

THE MASTER MAKES IT **ABSOLUTELY** CLEAR

110

Hegel argues that this process underpins the whole of history, and the history of thought. Early philosophers are part of the developing dialectical thought process that leads to knowledge and self-consciousness, and to the culmination of philosophy which appears to be the Hegelian system itself.

The system begins with "pure indeterminate being" and ends with the Absolute Idea or Truth itself. This Absolute Idea is like "thought thinking itself", or Aristotle's philosopher's God, the Unmoved Mover.

1 LOGICAL IDEA

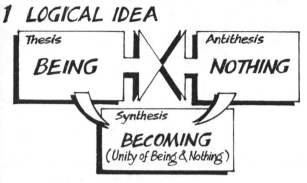

Thesis
BEING

Antithesis
NOTHING

Synthesis
BECOMING
(Unity of Being & Nothing)

Here is an historical example from the *"Philosophy of Right"* which shows how the **dialectic** operates in considering the notion of **right**:

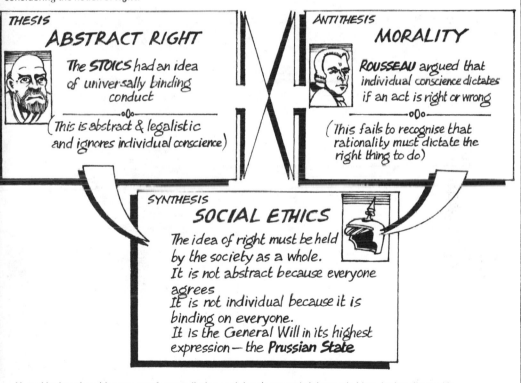

THESIS
ABSTRACT RIGHT

The **STOICS** had an idea of universally binding conduct
——o()o——
(This is abstract & legalistic and ignores individual conscience)

ANTITHESIS
MORALITY

ROUSSEAU argued that individual conscience dictates if an act is right or wrong
——o()o——
(This fails to recognise that rationality must dictate the right thing to do)

SYNTHESIS
SOCIAL ETHICS

The idea of right must be held by the society as a whole.
It is not abstract because everyone agrees
It is not individual because it is binding on everyone.
It is the General Will in its highest expression — the **Prussian State**

Hegel insists that this process of contradiction and development is inherent in historical reality and in thought, and that the working-out of these contradictions leads by necessity to the higher stages.

This should give you an idea of how the system works. How it all connects, and whether it is inevitable, or makes any sense — that's another matter.

2 PHILOSOPHY of NATURE

Hegel said Nature represented the Idea "outside itself". The Logical Idea, Nature & Spirit are, of course,   linked:

| Thesis **Logical Idea** Underlying all reality | Antithesis **Nature** Non-rational, outer aspect of same reality | Synthesis **Spirit** Unity of Idea & Nature |

3 PHILOSOPHY of SPIRIT

Here **Hegel** looks at what he considers the highest sphere — the workings of the Spirit throughout history. The dialectic looks like this:

| Thesis **Subjective Spirit** | Antithesis **Objective Spirit** | Synthesis **Absolute Spirit** |

This Spirit, (or Subject, or Reason, or Mind), which is objective as well as Absolute, rules the world. The Absolute Spirit or Absolute Idea unfolds through the ages and reveals itself absolutely to **Hegel**.
This was very convenient for **Hegel** as it allowed him to become a sort of Prussian philosopher-pope and to be buried with state honours when he went off to join the Absolute Spirit. It is not clear why the Absolute Spirit picked **Hegel** for this revelation.

| Subjective Spirit **Inner workings of the Human Mind** | Objective Spirit **Mind in its external embodiment in social & political institutions** | Absolute Spirit **Art, Religion, Philosophy** |

Hegel gives many examples to show that the Absolute is Spirit. More interestingly, he argues that this spirit is manifested in individuals, in social institutions like the family & the state, and in the art, religion & philosophy of an age.

This idea of the Objective Spirit as the external embodiment of the mind has been taken up by other philosophers. The notion of **ZEITGEIST** (literally Time-Spirit) — the inter-connections between individuals, society, art and religion in a particular age — has been extremely influential in modern history. The importance of understanding the totality, the system as a whole, clearly helped shape Marxism and much else besides.

The Zeit-Geist

Hegel then saw history as "the march of reason in the world" and human institutions as the product of the dialectical **becoming**. It may be possible to see how he related his Logic, Nature and Spirit to the Absolute Idea. It would probably look something like this:

The March of Reason

> I UNDERSTAND IT COMPLETELY NOW— EXCEPT FOR THE SYSTEM

THINGS TO REMEMBER ABOUT HEGEL'S SYSTEM

- *It is a system in motion*
- *Contradiction (the dialectic) is the motor*
- *The system is all-embracing*
- *The appearance of things (at rest) is different to their reality (in motion)*
- *All history is the working-out of the Spirit through time. This is the March of Reason*
- *Logic = metaphysics*

> I'VE FORGOTTEN THE EARLY BITS- CAN YOU REPEAT IT IN 50 WORDS?

Reality is constructed by **mind**. The **mind** doesn't know this at first. **Mind** thinks **reality** is out there, independent of it. Thus **mind** is alienated from itself. Then it recognises **reality** as its own creation. It then knows **reality** as clearly as it knows itself. It is at one with itself.

> THAT'S 51!

> MY DEAR DUCK, YOU SIMPLY HAVE TO REMEMBER THAT EVERY PART OF THE SYSTEM WORKS THROUGH THE PROCESS OF DEVELOPING SELF-CONSCIOUSNESS. TAKE WORLD HISTORY: IT STARTS WITH PURE BEING IN CHINA, DEVELOPS THRO' PARTIAL CONSCIOUSNESS IN THE GREEKS & ROMANS, AND ENDS WITH COMPLETE SELF-REALISATION IN THE HEGELIAN SYSTEM & THE PRUSSIAN STATE

Before leaving **Hegel** we should mention the enormous influence he had, and still *has*, on philosophy. There are Young Hegelians, Left Hegelians, New Hegelians and Old Hegelians. And there was his impact on MARX...

Marx was influenced by the radical and dynamic side of **Hegel**'s thinking, his dialectical method, but rejected his conservatism and idealism.

HEGEL ON BALANCE..

> THAT'S ALL FOLKS!

Interconnection of Thought & Society

The DIALECTIC

+

Absolute IDEALISM

Glorification of the Prussian State

Obscurity

Very few jokes

Hegel was the foremost of the early nineteenth century philosophers who constructed vast, complex systems claiming to reveal the secrets of man, nature and the universe. Hegelian idealism dominated German and much of European thought in this *"age of the system"*.

Oddly, **Hegel** and his followers made no real connections between their grand systems and the increasingly complex social and scientific shifts of their contemporary world.

While the **Young Hegelians** tried to popularise **Hegel**, **Schopenhauer** was steadfastly rejecting everything he had to say.

Arthur Schopenhauer
(1788 –1860)

comes over as the absolute antithesis of the whole German idealist movement. He disliked great systems, preferring a single thought. He rejected academic philosophy — his entertaining diatribe *On University Philosophy* is still worth reading. He attacked the **Hegelians'** metaphysics, their philosophy of religion and their German nationalism. Declaring himself an atheist, he looked back to the Enlightenment, and especially **Voltaire**.

HEGEL IS A STUPID AND CLUMSY CHARLATAN

During his short career as a University lecturer in Berlin he wrote his major work, *"The World as Will and Idea"*, which made little initial impact.

Schopenhauer starts from **Kant**, and says that the **thing-in-itself** corresponds to the **WILL**. This is his unique contribution to philosophy.

Kant, you will remember, distinguished between the world of appearances and the world of things-in-themselves which *he* said were unknowable.

Schopenhauer claims that we know the world of appearances through the operation of the will. The body is an appearance whose reality resides in the will, and through the immediate knowledge of the body we know the will. Then he develops this notion:

- The will is fundamental. Reason and sensations follow from it.
- The individual will is really only the one, universal will.
- This universal will is blind, irrational, and evil — and thus the source of all suffering.
- Only through *denial* of the will, through chastity, poverty, love and fasting can one achieve wisdom.

SOUNDS LIKE BUDDHISM TO ME

THE WILL RULES OK!

WE FOLLOW OUR FUTILE AIMS AS WE BLOW OUT A SOAP-BUBBLE AS LONG & AS LARGE AS POSSIBLE, ALTHOUGH WE KNOW PERFECTLY WELL THAT IT WILL BURST

Like other philosophers **Schopenhauer** believed in the difference between theory and practice. He ate and drank well, he philandered, he was occasionally rude and often greedy. He even pushed downstairs and seriously injured an elderly seamstress. His essay *On Women* argues points like
"You need only look at the way she is formed to see that woman is not meant to undergo great labour, whether of the mind or of the body".
Schopenhauer's idea of the **"primacy of the will"** influenced philosophers like **Nietzsche, Bergson, James** and **Dewey**. Outside philosophy it affected many Romantic artists and mystics, including **Wagner**, and perhaps most importantly, **Freud**.

The philosophically overcrowded nineteenth century could, at a stretch, be seen in terms of Hegel and anti-Hegel. Or between idealism and materialism.
Kierkegaard, the Danish pastor, hardly fits any of these categories however. In a way he doesn't really belong to the nineteenth century at all, being what you might call the **grandfather of existentialism**.

Søren **Kierkegaard**
(1813-1855)

was a rather strange person, by turn a cynic and a deeply religious thinker, who died rather young. Kierkegaard's major target was Hegel and his abstract universalizing system. To Kierkegaard Hegel attempted to capture all of reality in the net of his dialectic and real existence slipped through the holes. For Kierkegaard philosophy starts and finishes with the individual.

EXISTENCE IS A CATEGORY RELATING TO THE INDIVIDUAL..

.. NOT A UNIVERSAL IDEA

THE INDIVIDUAL MUST **ACT & CHOOSE** —THIS IS EXISTENCE

SO WHY DID YOU PUBLISH UNDER PSEUDONYMS?

WHAT IS TRUTH THEN?

TRUTH IS SUBJECTIVITY, NOT AXIOMS OR SYSTEMS

TRUTH IS AN OBJECTIVE UNCERTAINTY HELD FAST IN AN APPROPRIATION-PROCESS OF THE MOST PASSIONATE INWARDNESS

Oddly enough Kierkegaard remained a christian all his life and was also a witty, brilliant and entertaining writer and critic. Despite his deep concern for ethics and his idea of sympathy for others he acted in an appalling way towards the woman he was engaged to, announcing in public that his philosophical work was more important than marriage and therefore the engagement was dissolved. In his *'Stages in life's Way'* he wrote of woman, ***"She can only be rightly construed under the category of jest."***

1 Kierkegaard believed in a *lived* philosophy — he rejected Hegel's abstract idealism...

2 At first the individual explores the world of wit & sensuality — he is the AESTHETIC MAN typified by DON JUAN. But this is not enough....

116

3 He has to explore the world of moral responsibilities — he becomes the ETHICAL MAN typified by SOCRATES. But this is not enough...

4 After much travail, dread etc., he comes to the essence of subjectivity, a sort of rational suicide or LEAP of FAITH, & throws his lot in with eternity

First, the enormous & continuing influence of HEGEL …

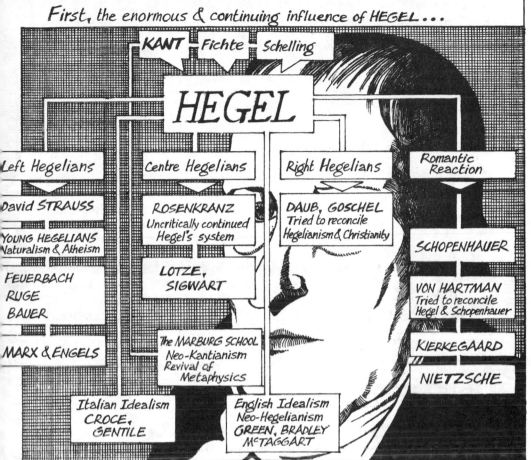

KANT Fichte Schelling

HEGEL

Left Hegelians	Centre Hegelians	Right Hegelians	Romantic Reaction
David STRAUSS	ROSENKRANZ Uncritically continued Hegel's system	DAUB, GOSCHEL Tried to reconcile Hegelianism & Christianity	
YOUNG HEGELIANS Naturalism & Atheism			SCHOPENHAUER
FEUERBACH RUGE BAUER	LOTZE, SIGWART		VON HARTMAN Tried to reconcile Hegel & Schopenhauer
MARX & ENGELS	The MARBURG SCHOOL Neo-Kantianism Revival of Metaphysics		KIERKEGAARD
			NIETZSCHE

Italian Idealism CROCE, GENTILE

English Idealism Neo-Hegelianism GREEN, BRADLEY MᶜTAGGART

This is just the **IDEALIST** side of thought. On the next page we look at the re-emergence of **MATERIALISM**.

SPOT THE MISSING PHILOSOPHER

You will have gathered by now that philosophically-speaking the nineteenth century was very busy. This makes it rather complicated, so we can't discuss everything, just some of the high spots, and the bits we like

ALL CHANGE!

Alongside idealism, and the continuing influence of Hegel's system-building there was a return to the ideas of the Enlightenment and thought based on material realities.

117

As everybody knows **MARXISM** was a major part of the return to materialism.

Everybody also knows that **MARX** was a complex philosopher who was influenced by German idealism, English political economy and French rationalism.

We'll start with the **YOUNG HEGELIANS** who denied the Christian implications of **Hegel**'s thought. The high point of Left Hegelian criticism of religion came with **David Strauss**'s *"Life of Jesus"* (1835), in which he argued that religion was no more than a myth in a particular historical form.

Bauer went further, and **Feuerbach** even further, rejecting the abstractions of Hegelian reason and replacing them with man as a concrete thinker in a social world.

Feuerbach (1804 - 1872)

In *"The Essence of Christianity"* **Feuerbach** talked about the "species life" of man, which he saw as particular to man because he lived a self-conscious social life. **Feuerbach** brought **Hegel** down to earth, and **Marx** then stood him on his head.

Marx's understanding of the realities of proletarian life was greatly enhanced by **Engels**' first-hand experience as manager in the textile business in Manchester, and his great work *"The Condition of the Working-Class in England"* (1844).

After the failed revolution of 1848, **Marx** ended up in London, where he remained for the rest of his life. Often he & his family lived in poverty, only eased by constant subs from **Engels**. That didn't stop him from studying and writing (and writing and writing).

LEND US ANOTHER FIVER FRED —WE'RE SKINT

120

In London **Marx** added to the last part of his great synthesis. This concerned economics — previously ignored or belittled by historians.

AS WELL AS THE INCREASING POLARISATION BETWEEN BOURGEOISIE & PROLETARIAT..

..STILL NEED TO EXPLAIN ALIENATION & MODE OF PRODUCTION MORE CLEARLY

It is worth pointing out here that **Marx**'s thought developed continually and that there are simply so many ideas in his collected works, many only published after his death, that it is rather difficult to say *"this is what Marx meant"*. Some people divide him into a young and an old Marx, some divide him from Engels and others divide the early humanist from the later historical materialist.

Possibly the *"Grundrisse"*, written in 1857-8, is the most significant turning-point. (It wasn't published in English until 1953.) In it he sorts out **Ricardo & Proudhon** and develops in outline the economic ideas that underpin the great work *"Capital"*.

THE BRITISH ECONOMISTS UNDERSTOOD SOMETHING.. **ADAM SMITH** SAW THAT INDUSTRIALISATION MEANT SHARPER & SHARPER DIVISIONS OF **LABOUR**, AND **RICARDO** FIRST PUT FORWARD A **LABOUR THEORY** OF **VALUE**, IN WHICH THE EXCHANGE VALUE OF A COMMODITY DEPENDS SIMPLY ON THE AMOUNT OF LABOUR SPENT ON IT

BUT THEY SANCTIFIED PRIVATE PROPERTY & TRIED TO JUSTIFY THE STATUS QUO. FOR THEM, HUMAN NATURE WAS FIXED & ABSTRACT. THE LIBERAL LAISSEZ-FAIRE MARKET ECONOMY ALLOWED THE MAXIMUM FREEDOM

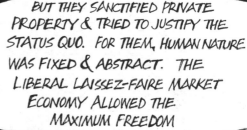

..AND THAT, WE KNOW, IS **RUBBISH**. FREE COMPETITION DOESN'T FREE INDIVIDUALS— IT MERELY SETS CAPITAL FREE TO EXPLOIT WORKERS!

RIGHT- THE APPEARANCE OF FREEDOM HIDES THE REALITY OF ALIENATION. OLD **PROUDHON** HALF KNEW THIS WHEN HE SAID *"PROPERTY IS THEFT"*, BUT HE FAILED TO THINK IT THROUGH

123

All wealth comes from labour.
So private property is the expropriation of the products of labour by one class from another.

Under capitalism it appears that wealth creates wealth.
Relations between individuals appear as relations between things.

Labour too appears as a thing, a commodity (labour-power), which the labourer sells to the capitalist in a supposedly free exchange.

The worker works to survive and the capitalist works to produce profit. Only the capitalist doesn't so much work as control the means of production.

The worker sells his labour-power for its value, which is the cost of its reproduction, but produces more than this, which is surplus value.

This surplus value is where the capitalist gets his profit. The key to it all is therefore the extraction of SURPLUS VALUE from abstract labour-power.

So **private property** and **alienation** are linked for **Marx** in a system which seems to create freedom (the freedom of the market-place), but which enslaves people within the world of objects or commodities.
Men and women have become **objects** for each other, unable to see the reality of capitalism as a system.
They *imagine* they are free, and project the appearance of freedom into their ideas, creating an ideology, but **...**

IT IS NOT THE CONSCIOUSNESS OF HUMAN BEINGS WHICH DETERMINES THEIR BEING, BUT, ON THE CONTRARY, THEIR SOCIAL BEING WHICH DETERMINES THEIR CONSCIOUSNESS

Friedrich Nietzsche
(1844 – 1900)

WHAT I UNDERSTAND BY 'PHILOSOPHER': A **TERRIBLE EXPLOSIVE** IN THE PRESENCE OF WHICH EVERYTHING IS IN **DANGER**

is one of those philosophers who has entered the mainstream of cultural life as a caricature, an eccentric who said "God is Dead", invented supermen, and, probably, Nazism. In reality he's more complex, in fact much more complex.

Nietzsche was a brilliant student who was appointed professor of classics at Basel University when he was only 24. He suffered from chronic ill-health which may, or may not, have been psychosomatic. He took drugs, argued with almost everyone, wandered Europe in increasing isolation and finally went mad in 1889 for reasons that are much discussed. His love of **Wagner**, misogyny, hatred of Christianity & anti-democratic ethics are also well known.

As well as a philosopher, **Nietzsche** was a poet, a great stylist and rhetorician, and much given to aphorisms. This has led to many different interpretations of his work. His influence has been enormous, contradictory and not confined to philosophy. Above all, though, he addressed the central problem of modern man – prey to nihilism – adrift in a complex society in which God was dying, if not dead.

We'll look at some of the **Nietzsches** who made up this fragmented semi-tortured thinker who opposed philosophical system-building as false.

Nietzsche 1

THIS WAS MY GREEK/WAGNERIAN PERIOD IN WHICH I WROTE "THE BIRTH OF TRAGEDY"

SCHOPENHAUER'S ATHEISM & ANTI-RATIONALISM INFLUENCED ME GREATLY

GERMAN CULTURE, LIKE GREEK CULTURE AFTER SOCRATES, WAS DECADENT & PHILISTINE . IT COULD ONLY BE SAVED BY WAGNER

125

I REJECTED WAGNER WHEN HE BECAME A BORN-AGAIN CHRISTIAN

THIS WAS A CONSISTENT PROJECT IN MY WORK — IT IS **FALSE** TO TRY & DIVIDE ME UP

..BUT CONTINUED MY SEARCH FOR A MORALITY TO REPLACE THE ONE GREAT CURSE, THAT ENORMOUS & INNERMOST PERVERSION — **CHRISTIANITY**

FROM BEGINNING TO END I SOUGHT TO APPLY THE KNIFE VIVISECTIONALLY TO THE VERY VIRTUES OF THE TIME

I MAY HAVE **PLAYED** THE RATIONALIST FOR A WHILE..

..BUT I REALISED MY OWN PHASES WERE JUST **MASKS**

..OR SELF-ADMINISTERED **TONICS** WHICH HELPED ME TO HIGHER THOUGHTS

ism Nº7

Neitzsche has a point here — so perhaps we shold look at his central ideas. But bear in mind that he, like **Heraclitus,** saw everything as being in a state of flux, even though later he took up the idea of ETERNAL RECURRENCE.

126

In his work on Greek tragedy **Nietzsche** made an important distinction between the two gods, **Apollo** & **Dionysius.**

Apollo was the symbol of order, form and restraint.

Dionysius was the symbol of the frenzy of passion & of vital forces.

Nietzsche explained Greek tragedy as the conquest of **Dionysius** by **Apollo,** and art as the product of this dynamic conflict.

For **Nietzsche,** 19th century culture denied the Dionysian, smothering everything with life-denying Christian pieties, and was incapable of providing man with a real moral basis.

WE MUST GO BEYOND THE SIMPLE CHRISTIAN IDEA OF **GOOD** & **EVIL**

THERE IS **NO** UNIVERSAL MORALITY

MEN ARE INDIVIDUALS & MUST BE JUDGED AS SUCH

CHRISTIANITY IS THE MORALITY OF PALTRY PEOPLE AS THE MEASURE OF ALL THINGS **!!**

IT IS THE MORALITY OF THE **HERD,** A **SLAVE** MORALITY **!**

Much of this is expressed in **Nietzsche's** best-known work, ***"Thus Spake Zarathustra."***
This extraordinary poetic book, a kind of metaphoric prophecy of his ideas, is as much literature as philosophy. Here he talks of that man. the ÜBERMENSCH (SUPERMAN) who desires through his will to power, which for him is just the will to live, a higher, more powerful state of being. He, the Übermensch, was to be judged differently from ordinary mortals. Out of the total revaluation of all morals the 'noble man' would emerge, a man of strength, hardness and, if need be, cruelty.

Some people argue that the brilliance of **Nietzsche's** style make plausible what are essentially weird ideas, but this is to mistake his love of paradox and prophecy. Mind you, in ***"Zarathustra"*** he does say at one point:

"Man shall be trained for war and women for the recreation of the warrier. All else is folly."

Where **Marx** had said the future lay with the masses, **Nietzsche** stood this on its head to assert that the future lay with great men. He saw the masses as necessary, but only as the foundation for these higher men. He saw his Superman as the *goal of life,* or even a *myth.* He gave as example **Socrates,** a passionate man whose passions were under control, but added to him an artistic temperament. Elsewhere he indicates that his Superman is like **Aristotle's** ethical ideal, the 'great-souled man'.

128

" *I teach you the Superman...man is something to be surpassed*
Man is a rope connecting animal & superman — a rope over a precipice ...
What is great in man is that he is a bridge and not a goal"

Nietzsche's radically different views about human nature marked a significant shift in the history of philosophy. The idea of the rational subject was rejected in favour of a much more complex, and psychologically based view of man and morality. The rational basis of morality Nietzsche thought was an illusion.

What is particularly interesting about all of **Nietzsche's** work is the way in which he decisively does away with the common-sense notion of rational man. He understands "sublimation" and how the repression of sexual instincts drives irrationality, both in Christianity and in politics and morality. The "will to power" is the other side of instinct and its suppression. **Freud** recognised his genius in this respect.

NIETZSCHE'S PREMONITIONS & INSIGHTS ARE EXTRAORDINARY IN THE WAY THEY AGREE WITH PSYCHOANALYSIS

HE UNDERSTOOD THE RÔLE OF THE PASSIONS IN SUPPOSEDLY CIVILISED MAN & THE PSYCHOLOGICAL RÔLE OF RELIGION

HE ALSO UNDERSTOOD THE DYNAMIC DRIVES THAT UNDERLIE ARTISTIC ENDEAVOUR

129

Nietzsche was at his most uncannily prophetic when he talked about the advent of nihilism, and the inevitable backlash of complacent nineteenth-century culture:

> OUT OF THE DEATH OF GOD WILL COME AN ACTIVE NIHILISM & THE RISE OF SUPERMEN. THERE WILL BE **WARS** SUCH AS THERE HAVE NEVER BEEN ON EARTH BEFORE

> ONLY FROM MY TIME ON WILL THERE BE **POLITICS** ON THE GRAND SCALE

He was certainly right about that one, but perhaps not so right about the 'Supermen' who were to inherit his ideas. The aphoristic writer always gets misquoted.

> IS NOT LIFE A HUNDRED TIMES TOO SHORT FOR US TO **BORE OURSELVES?**

> THE **FUTURE** INFLUENCES THE PRESENT AS MUCH AS THE **PAST**

His other works *"Human, All-too Human", "The Anti-Christ", "The Genealogy of Morals", "Dawn", "The Gay Science"* and his *posthumous* **Notebooks** covered a lot more ground than the Superman debate.

He attacked the need for metaphysics as springing from physiological weakness, from a refusal to comfort the Cosmos through Will. He discussed what we now call the sociology of knowledge and developed a 'perspective' theory of truth.

> TRUTH, LIKE MORALITY, IS A RELATIVE AFFAIR: THERE ARE NO FACTS, ONLY INTERPRETATIONS

> LANGUAGE FALSIFIES REALITY

130

In science, sociology, existentialism and even analytic philosophy **Nietzsche** has had an influence that belies the tag 'eccentric'. He is probably less often read than read about. His irony, violent prejudices, brilliant style and occasional megalomania make him difficult and dangerous to read, but endlessly entertaining.

He died in 1900 (conveniently for historians) insane, isolated, but increasingly famous.

Back in England, where empiricism and a profound disinterest in European philosophy were rife, the effect of **Hegel** was practically nil. Instead, what was being developed was that peculiarly English common-sense philosophy: **UTILITARIANISM.**
It dominated the thinking of most Englishmen for most of the 19th century. One critic said that utilitarianism was no more than empiricism attempting to hold off the 20th century by imitating the 18th, whatever that means.

THE MORE WEALTH **WE** CREATE, THE HAPPIER **EVERYONE** IS

THAT'S A PHILOSOPHY?

UTILITARIANISM HOLDS THAT ACTIONS ARE **RIGHT** IN PROPORTION AS THEY TEND TO PROMOTE HAPPINESS, **WRONG** AS THEY TEND TO PRODUCE THE REVERSE OF HAPPINESS

J.S. Mill

131

..BY **HAPPINESS** IS INTENDED **PLEASURE** & THE ABSENCE OF PAIN, BY UNHAPPINESS, **PAIN** & THE PRIVATION OF PLEASURE

Jeremy Bentham
(1748 - 1832)

gave the first full outline in his *"Introduction to the Principles of Morals & Legislation"*

> NATURE HAS PLACED MANKIND UNDER THE GOVERNANCE OF TWO SOVEREIGN MASTERS, **PAIN & PLEASURE**

From these two masters he worked out a *'hedonic calculus'* with which to analyse actions both legally and socially. It was a liberal, reasonable approach to things: Bentham thought the civil law, through reform, would make everyone secure, equal and peaceful.

A strange bird, Bentham argued that all punishment was evil, yet designed prisons. A militant atheist, he left orders to be stuffed & placed in a glass box in the hall of the college he helped found

John Stuart Mill
(1806 - 1873)

inherited the ideas of Utilitarianism from his father **James Mill,** an ardent disciple of **Bentham,** as well as his father's strict ideas on education and everything else. Such was the effect of **James** on his son **John,** the young **Mill** fell into a "dull state of nerves" at the age of twenty, from which he only recovered by falling in love with a Mrs Taylor.

The son, like the father, wrote an important work on political economy. Both works, derived from **Ricardo** may well have influenced **Marx.**

The younger **Mill's** *"Utilitarianism"* was extremely influential. It defended the principle of utility, but in a way which modified **Bentham's** ideas.
Mill argued that pleasure could not be measured as a quantity, like coal, and went so far as to say that he would rather be a dissatisfied human being than a satisfied pig. He meant that pleasure is *qualitatively* as well as *quantitatively* different.
He thought altruism was as important as self-interest in deciding what ought to be done, and so turned from **Bentham's** external standard of Goodness towards something more subjective.

132

> OBLIGATION, I THINK, CAN BE COMPATIBLE WITH SELF-INTEREST PROVIDED IT LEADS TO THE **GREATEST GOOD** FOR THE **GREATEST NUMBER** OF PEOPLE

Utilitarianism seems like a workable functional morality but it has some serious problems:—

1. *It doesn't work in practice. How do you tell who is and who isn't happy?*
2. *How do you work out what produces happiness?*
3. *If you're part of a minority that has to be crushed in order to make the majority happy, it can get tiresome.*
4. *Utilitarianism looks at actions and their consequences, and disregards the enormously complicating question of motives.*

Problem 1

Problem 3

> IT'S FOR THE GREATEST GOOD

> UTILITARIANISM IS A TYPICALLY ENGLISH "COMMON-SENSE" BOTCH-UP AIMED AT JUSTIFYING LAISSEZ-FAIRE **GREED** WHILE SEEMING AS FUNCTIONAL & EFFICIENT AS THE NEW FACTORIES

> THAT'S A TYPICALLY CRUDE MARXIST GIBE

J S Mill wrote much on topics other than Utilitarianism. Philosophically he is remembered for his *"System of Logic"*, where he outlines the limits and nature of meaningful discussion, and which is still influential. His *"On Liberty"* is even more famous. Here he related individual liberties to those of the state, and argued that civil restrictions on individual liberties were only permissible if they were absolutely necessary to prevent harm to others.

> FREEDOM OF SPEECH & FREEDOM OF POLITICAL THOUGHT, THE EMANCIPATION OF WOMEN, & EQUALITY BEFORE THE LAW ARE ALL GOOD UTILITARIAN PRINCIPLES

133

In the intellectual turmoil of early 19th century France there were many different strands of thought. Comte added a wholly new one that concentrated on the positive method of looking at the connection between observable facts.

Auguste Comte
(1798 – 1857)

Comte wanted to create a synthesis of thought and action but, like others before him, he held very contradictory ideas. In his early days he developed his science of society, or **sociology**, and in his later days his **religion of humanity,** which was a sort of secular Christianity based on an abstract Supreme Being. Comte himself recognized the contradictions at times.

He was for some years secretary to the well-known utopian socialist **Saint-Simon**, whom Comte probably influenced more than the other way around. Never obtaining an academic post, he was supported by friends, including **J.S.Mill**, throughout his life. Saint-Simon helped publish his *Plan of the Scientific Works Necessary for the Re-organization of Society*. The basic ideas of Comte's **positive philosophy** are outlined in this work and somewhat amplified in the six-volume *Course in Positive Philosophy*, published between 1830 and 1842.

DEFINE YOUR "POSITIVE PHILOSOPHY," AUGUSTE

WELL, IT ISN'T A METAPHYSICAL SYSTEM, NOR IS IT AN EXPLANATION OF ESSENCES

COULDN'T YOU BE MORE POSITIVE?

IT LOOKS ONLY AT FACTS & USES ONLY SCIENTIFIC METHODS

SO SCIENCE IS ALL-IMPORTANT & METAPHYSICS IS BUNK, EH?

YES — I'M POSITIVE ABOUT THAT ONLY SCIENCE CAN BE OF REAL BENEFIT TO SOCIETY

DON'T BENTHAM & MILL & OTHERS THINK SIMILARLY?

INDEED — MY FRIEND MILL SAYS POSITIVISM IS THE GENERAL PROPERTY OF THE AGE

POSITIVISM set out to be rigorous. Its basic tenets were:

1. In Nature there are laws that can be known
2. In Nature the causes of things <u>cannot</u> be known
3. Any proposition which cannot ultimately be reduced to a simple statement of fact, special or general, can have no real or intelligible sense
4. Only relations between facts can be known
5. Intellectual development is the primary cause of social change

The entire field of scientific study was arranged logically by COMTE. Each science contributes to those that follow in order, but not to those that precede it

	Logical Order	Order in which knowledge is actually gained
MATHEMATICS	1	6
ASTRONOMY	2	5
PHYSICS	3	4
CHEMISTRY	4	3
BIOLOGY	5	2
SOCIOLOGY	6	1

Comte argued in his *Law of the Three States* that the human mind advances from a **theological** stage through a **metaphysical** stage to a final **positive** stage (this has an Hegelian ring to it). He claimed that all the sciences developed in this way. To each stage of intellectual development Comte said there corresponds a form of society and outlook. (This idea, differently expressed, was widespread in 19th Century thought).

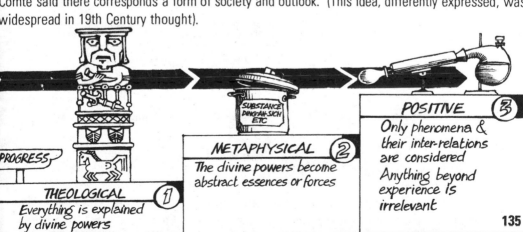

PROGRESS

THEOLOGICAL ① Everything is explained by divine powers

METAPHYSICAL ② The divine powers become abstract essences or forces

POSITIVE ③ Only phenomena & their inter-relations are considered. Anything beyond experience is irrelevant

135

Comte was ignored by almost everybody at the time. But the history of philosophy is always being re-written. Issues that once seemed important turn out not to be, and vice versa. **Herbert Spencer's evolutionism** once dominated nineteenth-century thinking, but now seems relatively unimportant. Where **Marx** was ignored **Spencer** was widely read, but now people think Spencer was part of the chain-store Marks & Spencer (some of them think **Marx** was too). **Comte** was like **Marx** in being ahead of his time, unlike **Marx** he was never to be caught up by it.

Herbert Spencer
(1820-1903)

was a man of many parts: engineer, teacher, journalist, and philosopher. His *System of Synthetic Philosphy* was a survey of the biological and social sciences from the standpoint of evolutionism. **Spencer** claimed that philosophy was distinguished from other sciences in being wholly general. By this he meant that its central ideas were true of everything, not just one field. Naturally he thought his principle of evolutionism was the central idea of philosophy, and true of everything. In *First Principles* , the first of many volumes on many subjects, Spencer outlined his law of evolution.

EVERYTHING PROGRESSES FROM AN INDEFINITE INCOHERENT HOMOGENEITY TO A DEFINITE COHERENT HETEROGENEITY

136

HOW COULD HE DO THAT BEFORE I'D WRITTEN THE "ORIGIN of SPECIES" IN 1859 ?

OUR IDEAS WEREN'T IDENTICAL... ANYWAY, MY "PRINCIPLES of PSYCHOLOGY" CAME OUT IN 1852

Charles **Darwin** (1809 - 82)

.. MAYBE YOUR IDEAS EVOLVED FROM MINE

It is difficult from this to see quite why **Spencer** had such an impact on 19th Century thought. But in effect it was because he argued for a kind of Social Darwinism.
Although it was Spencer who coined the phrase **survival of the fittest**, it was **Darwin's** detailed explanation of the principle that made evolutionism popular. And the notion that man and the higher apes had a common ancestor led to a new formulation of the idea of man.

Darwin argued that nature evolved according to the principle of **natural selection**. Each organism undergoes small accidental genetic variations in each generation. The organism with the variations which help it adapt best to the environment is the one most likely to survive.

Prince **Kropotkin**
(1842-1921)

MUTUAL AID IS JUST AS VITAL A PRINCIPLE IN NATURE

*A right old anarchist with a long beard.
A sort of Darwinian anarchist.*

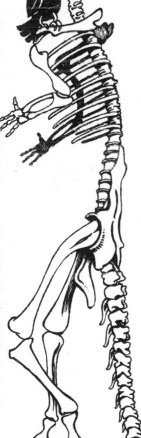

YOU'RE NOT ADAPTING

Spencer went further and argued that this natural selection process was the guiding force of <u>social</u> development too. Metaphysics and moral systems were just irrelevant. This suited the frame of mind of Victorian capitalists, and fitted in nicely with ideas of free economic competition dating back to **Adam Smith**.

He made a detailed comparison between animal organisms and human societies:

In an animal, there is one overall consciousness, but in society consciousness exists only in each member. Society exists for the benefit of the individual, not vice versa. This individualism is the key to **Spencer**. So he disliked the reforming Liberals of his time, arguing that true liberalism's function was only to put a limit to the power of Parliaments.

The philosophical **Radicals** took to Spencer's evolutionism, because it argued progress as a necessity, but it was his notion of societies evolving according to the survival of the fittest principle that had the most lasting influence. The idea was picked up by **Nietzsche** with his Superman, the **Eugenics** movement with their theory of scientific race-improvement, and even **Hitler** with the superior Aryan race.

The idea of an overlap between the natural and the human world has always had a strong attraction, and has re-appeared recently in what is known as socio-biology.

While European philosophy was busy splitting up into Idealists vs. Materialists, Hegelians and positivists etc., American philosophy had only just started. Since they had a new country (borrowed from the Indians) they thought they'd better have a new philosophy as well. Their major contribution, which emerged in the Nineteenth century, was.......

While Wild Bill Hickock was roaming the plains, C.S. Pierce was honing his thoughts, and in 1878 came up with the following:

C.S. Peirce
(1839-1914)

Consider what effects, which might conceivably have practical bearings, we conceive the object of our conception to have. Then our conception of these effects is the whole of our conception of the object.

This was simply meant to be a logical maxim for working out the meaning of words and concepts according to their practical significance. Or, in other words, to establish the relationship between thought and action.

138

QUITE— WE CAN SAY YOU'RE **DEAD**, WHICH IS TESTABLE, BUT NOT THAT YOU'RE A **SPIRIT**...

IT IS ASTONISHING TO SEE HOW MANY PHILOSOPHICAL DISPUTES COLLAPSE INTO INSIGNIFICANCE THE MOMENT YOU SUBJECT THEM TO THIS SIMPLE TEST OF TRACING A CONCRETE CONSEQUENCE

IN FACT, ALMOST EVERY PROPOSITION OF ONTOLOGICAL METAPHYSICS IS EITHER MEANINGLESS GIBBERISH OR ELSE DOWNRIGHT ABSURD...

Other people borrowed Pierce's ideas and turned them from a **theory of meaning** into a **general theory of truth** and a **pragmatic philosophy**. These cowboys were **William James, Ferdinand Schiller,** and **John Dewey. James** summed up the new version in his *Pragmatism*.

IDEAS BECOME TRUE JUST SO FAR AS THEY HELP US TO GET INTO SATISFACTORY RELATIONS WITH OTHER PARTS OF OUR EXPERIENCE

WHAT, IN SHORT, IS THE TRUTH'S CASH-VALUE IN EXPERIENTIAL TERMS? WHAT DOES IT DO FOR YOU?

William James
(1842–1910)

This version of pragmatism comes to be a down-to-earth way of saying that thoughts are just tools with which to do things, and truth what is pragmatically useful.

SO, WHAT'S PHILOSOPHY **GOOD FOR**? CAN YOU DRILL A HOLE WITH IT?

UM, NO— PRAGMATISM IS JUST A METHOD: IT DOESN'T PARTICULARLY TELL YOU ANYTHING

139

John Dewey turned this pragmatism into an ethical and educational philosophy which greatly influenced American social policy, particularly the legal and educational fields. Dewey synthesized the work of James and Pierce and came up with the idea of **Instrumentalism.**

John Dewey
(1859-1952)

IT'S MORE OR LESS THE SAME THING, JUST EMPHASISING THAT THOUGHTS ARE **INSTRUMENTAL** IN WORKING OUT PROBLEMS

AS MY OLD FRIEND WILLIAM JAMES SAID THE OLD SUBJECT-OBJECT DUALISM IS DEAD... THINKING IS REALLY A PROCESS OF ADJUSTMENT BETWEEN MAN & HIS ENVIRONMENT

TRUTH IS A RELATIVE THING THAT IS WORKED OUT THROUGH EXPERIENCE, THROUGH LIFE.

Throughout his long life, Dewey believed that intelligence, behavior and knowledge could change, and that therefore education was crucial to shaping society. Pragmatism had a major influence in this area, arguing for experimental problem-solving and non-dogmatic teaching. The problem with Pragmatism is that by saying that everything is relative, like truth, one can never decide anything philosophically. Other people have said that Pragmatism fits in very well with the efficiency of industrial capitalism, which is why Americans liked it.

From C.S. Peirce on there had been a pragmatic feel to American philosophy, a sort of reasonableness that was in between scepticism and dogmatism. In some ways this strand continued into twentieth-century American philosophy.

Dewey in **Reconstruction of Philosophy** (1920) had another go at applying pragmatist views to every-thing. (Pragmatism is clearly good for you since Dewey lived for a very long time.) Instrumentalism, which is much the same thing, lived on for a long time as well. It says that ultimately whether ideas are true or false is not a serious question, it's just a question of how useful they are. **Richard Rorty**, another American philoso-pher, now seems to be saying the same thing.

As American philosophers get older they seem to turn to pragmatism, but it is not self-evident which deter-mines which. Just to mess up the pattern **George Santayana** (1863-1952) lived for a long time but hated pragmatism. He was a thorough-going sceptic, believed in Platonic universals (or 'essences') and somehow combined this with a sort of naturalistic realism. He was also a poet and cultural critic who hated man, culture and democracy in general. Definitely an individualist he also disliked Protestants, was probably only a part-time American and ended his days in Rome.

John Rawls (1921-)

is not all that old and therefore not entirely a pragmatist, if at all, but he might become one. He is mainly famous for **A Theory of Justice** (1971) in which he is very concerned with individual rights; he tried to develop a notion of 'justice as fairness', something which is very topical in the States right now.

Rawls reintroduced the notion of a 'social contract' (as found in Rousseau and Locke). and suggested that this was based on rational agreements about how to achieve justice. Rawls pragmatically suggests that no-one should be better off than anyone else and that inequality is not at all a good, or natural, thing. Needless to say lots of people vehemently disagree with him. **Nozick**, a radical libertarian (which is philosophy-speak for right-winger) set out to demolish Rawls in **Anarchy, State and Utopia**.

Willard V O Quine

(1908-)

is America's answer to
Wittgenstein, analytic philosophy
and continental obscurity. He
carries Ockham's razor around in
his pocket with him, ready to slice
up confusion and unnecessary
complexity.

Although he started out as a logical
positivist, with that firm notion that
bits of empirical proposition tallied
with bits of experience, he soon
decided there was 'less to it than
meets the eye'. He saw off what he
called the dogmas of empiricism
and came to an interesting and
complicated conclusion that
science, experience and common-
sense were all bound up in a 'web
of knowledge'.

This actually makes philosophy quite difficult since Quine points to the inter-connectedness and corporate
nature of different forms of knowledge. (Sounds like pragmatism to me.) This means that he is sceptical
about finding singular items of meaning, the basic unit is all of science.

Put another way this all pointed to the great
difficulties we all have with language and
meaning, although Quine does seem to propose
the perfect philosopher as an intellectual spider
man. It points to the way continental philosophy
got interested in language too, but it is a unique
American approach. Although it doesn't sound
like it, Quine is very funny, a writer with a wit
that would put Kant in a tizz.

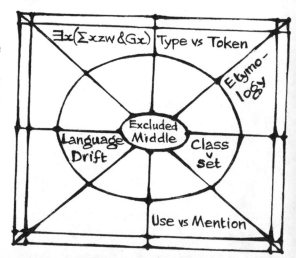

By the end of the Nineteenth Century philosophy hadn't solved all the problems it had set out to, and most of the great philosophical systems seemed to be crumbling away. Scientific modes of thought were everywhere, from Newtonian cosmology to the biological determinism of evolutionary theory. Kantian and Hegelian philosophy still survived, but science was more authoritative.

Then a wave of anti-intellectualism broke over Western philosophy, rejecting rationality and scientific analysis.

Henri Bergson
(1859 - 1900)

Henri Bergson was central in all this. He was appointed Professor of Modern Philosophy at the College de France in 1900, so we can call him a 20th Century Philosopher.

YOU COULD ALSO CALL HIM AN IRRATIONALIST, A METAPHYSICIAN, A DUALIST, & A CREATIVE EVOLUTIONIST..

SCIENCE ONLY ANALYSES IT DOESN'T GET TO THE DYNAMIC VITAL ESSENCE ... IT DISSECTS & SEPARATES THE ORGANIC, LIVING REALITY

Bergson rejected the idea that science was the main source of knowledge, and claimed that intuition was more important. This notion clearly goes back to the **Romantics** and **Rousseau**.

Bergson's philosophy is dynamic and dualist.

143

On the one hand : **Inert Matter**

On the other : *A vast vital impulse*

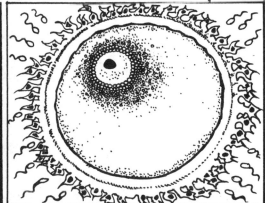

Life (**élan vital**) manifests itself in many forms, in a struggle against matter, and, for Bergson, this is what drives "creative evolution" along.

> THE UNIVERSE HAS TWO TENDENCIES, A REALITY WHICH IS **MAKING** ITSELF IN A REALITY WHICH IS **UNMAKING** ITSELF

> THE ONE IS LIFE, & THE OTHER IS MATTER, WHICH IS OPPOSED TO LIFE

Bergson said that thinking was like the universe: on the one hand intuition which draws from the life force, and on the other analysis, which draws from an artificially-fixed system based on matter.

Bergson's book *Creative Evolution* (1907) was extremely influential in its day, in literature as well as in philosophy. His ideas on time are well known through Proust. Although many people claim he is obscure and metaphoric, he has had a lasting influence on criticism of the sciences, and on philosophies of life and action. Georges Sorel attempted to unify revolutionary syndicalism and Bergson's thought. G. Bernard Shaw was also influenced by what he saw as Bergson's 'vitalism'

> THE ONLY TRUE PARADISES ARE THE PARADISES WE HAVE LOST

Sigmund Freud
(1856-1939)

Someone else who put a spanner in the smooth workings of philosophy was the founder of psychoanalysis, Sigmund Freud

> IN THE MAIN, I SIMPLY DISCOVERED THE **UNCONSCIOUS**, UNDERMINED CARTESIAN RATIONALITY & POSED A NEW CONCEPTION OF HUMAN NATURE & CIVILISATION

> IS HE A PHILOSOPHER?

> ..A POET?

> ...A SCIENTIST?

144

There is a large debate about whether Psychoanalysis is a science and whether Freud was right about human sexual development and the Unconscious. The revolutionary importance of his ideas derived from his insistence on the centrality of sexuality in all aspects of human existence. This also explained in part why his ideas were resisted. (see *Freud for Beginners*).

These ideas obviously posed many problems for philosophy, which tends to assume rationality as a given when talking about how people think and know things. Freud's ideas about human sexuality, culture and aggression also tended to make life difficult for social and moral theorists. Many philosophers have opted for the line that since psychoanalysis isn't empirically testable (you can't photograph the Unconscious), Freud can safely be ignored.

From Pierce and Pragmatism to Nietzsche and Nihilism the 19th Century saw philosophy getting more divided about what it could achieve. The complexity of industrial capitalist society, and the rapid pace of change and development, made social thought, and philosophy, more complicated. Marx had declared the end of philosophy, whilst Nietzsche and Bergson had respectively destroyed it and recreated it.

The late 19th Century was in desperate need of someone to point the way out of the philosophical maelstrom and failed to recognise him in the figure of **Gottlob Frege**. It was realised after Frege's death that he was the founder of modern logic, mathematical logic, and what is now called 'analytical philosophy'. Frege rejected epistemology as the starting point of philosophy (which reversed most things since Descartes) and attempted to put logic back in the driving seat.

Gottlob Frege
(1848–1925)

HE REMAINED WHOLLY WITHOUT RECOGNITION UNTIL *I* DREW ATTENTION TO HIM

THEN WHITEHEAD & MYSELF, THE HUMBLE BERTIE RUSSELL, TRIED TO PROVE THAT PURE MATHEMATICS IS ONLY A PART OF **LOGIC**

Principia Mathematica

* Frege put mathematics on a new and more solid foundation.
+
* He purged mathematics of mistaken, sloppy reasoning and the influence of Pythagoras
+
* He gave a new, rigorous definition of numbers (equinumerosity)
+
* He showed that Kant's theory of mathematical propositions as 'synthetic a priori' was wrong
=
A Revolution in Logic
If we divide this up into straightforward bits, minus the much-too-hard mathematical proofs of things,
We get the following:

MATHEMATICS IS NOT A MYSTICAL, SEPARATE ENTITY

IT IS SIMPLY A PROJECTION OF OUR ABILITY TO THINK CLEARLY, SIMPLY A BRANCH OF LOGIC

147

Two important theses followed from this sense/reference distinction:
1. The meaning of a given sentence must be derived from the meaning of its parts
2. Only in the context of whole sentences does any word have a definite meaning

Frege's attempt to mechanise the thought-processes of reasoning, to clean up the act of thinking, was not entirely new. Nor was the link between mathematics and philosophy. Really the project had begun long before with **Aristotle's** syllogisms and **Euclid's** geometry. In the 19th Century logicians like **Boole** and **de Morgan** and a new breed of mathematicians like **Cantor** and **Peano** had helped set the scene for Frege.

Following Frege, **Russell** and **Whitehead** tried to tidy up mathematics once and for all. But in trying to find a logical definition of number, in terms of classes, Russell ran up against a paradox.

(A paradox is something that happens in philosophy all the time. It is the epistemological version of Sod's Law which means that if you think you've just solved all the problems you suddenly discover that they didn't exist.)

Whitehead

RUSSELL's PARADOX

Most classes don't contain themselves as members – e.g. the class of all walruses is not a walrus. Some do. But consider THE CLASS OF ALL CLASSES THAT ARE NOT MEMBERS OF THEMSELVES. Is **it** a member of itself or not?
If you think about it, it is if it isn't and isn't if it is...

Poor old **Frege** gave up at this point, whereas **Russell** tried again with his theory of types, to banish these strange loops arising fron self-reference. But then in 1931, **Kurt Gödel** came up with his famous Incompleteness Theorem which devastated the whole project.

Kurt Gödel

IN ANY SYSTEM CONTAINING ARITHMETIC, THERE ARE TRUE STATEMENTS WHICH CANNOT BE PROVED WITHIN THE SYSTEM

I'm true

..and I'm outside the SYSTEM

The logical analysis begun by **Frege** led to the school of thought which is called **analytic philosophy**, and which is still popular today. As a school it has many strands. All are based on the new logic and share the **analytic** approach stemming from **Frege, Russell, and Wittgenstein.**

Characteristic of the school is the desire to clarify, through analysis, and a hostility toward metaphysics.

Some of the strands:

| The Vienna Circle Schlick Carnap **LOGICAL POSITIVISM** | Russell Wittgenstein **LOGICAL ATOMISM** | Russell Whitehead Gödel **LOGICISM** | Wittgenstein **ORDINARY LANGUAGE PHILOSOPHY** | BAD LANGUAGE PHILOSOPHY ? |

Ludwig Wittgenstein
(1889–1951)

MY DREAM WAS TO CREATE A PERFECT, LOGICAL LANGUAGE ABLE TO STATE EVERYTHING WITH THE UTMOST PRECISION

Wittgenstein was important to all these phases. His *Tractatus Logico-Philosophicus* (1921) claimed to solve all the problems of philosophy.

IN THE TRACTATUS I ARGUED THAT EVERYTHING THAT COULD BE **THOUGHT** COULD ALSO BE **SAID**

149

..WHEREAS NOTHING CAN BE SAID ABOUT SOMETHING, LIKE GOD, THAT CAN'T BE PROPERLY THOUGHT... PHILOSOPHY IS CLARITY

Somebody called Carnap said that all philosophical problems were really syntactical. If you sort out the syntax of what you're saying most philosophical problems are either solved or shown to be insoluble. This sounds like if you're clear then philosophy is either sorted out or non-existent.

Wittgenstein first said that the world consisted of simple facts (like atoms - hence logical atomism) and the world is made up of a lot of them. Then he said that language could only be used to picture facts or to make logical statements. Next he argued that any use of language other than the above is meaningless. All ethical or metaphysical statements are therefore nonsense.

Hence, his own theory of language is meaningless because it tries to show how abstract relationships in language work. (In other words, the project of a perfect, formal language is impossible!) If you understand Wittgenstein you'll give up philosophy.

ut of Wittgenstein also came the **logical positivists** who were otherwise known as the Vienna ircle. They held certain views in common, some tea dances, and a journal called *Erkenntnis*.

There was *Carnap & Schlick,*
Weissman & Frank,
Kraft, Kaufmann & Feigl;

They all adored logic,
As well as analysis,
And totally hated **Hegel**

This introduced the famous Verification Principle, which Karl Popper turned into his own Falsification Thesis.

" *The meaning of a proposition is the method of its verification* "

1. A proposition has meaning only if it can be shown to be true or false.
2. There are logical forms of truth and factual forms.
3. Factual truths can only be demonstrated through experience (verification).

YOU CAN'T BELIEVE SOMETHING UNLESS IT IS FALSIFIABLE

TRUE OR FALSE?

The logical positivists didn't give up philosophy like Wittgenstein but went on doing 'analysis' all over the world. Failure to solve its problems about how language does work however, led to logical positivism going round in circles.

Wittgenstein made his philosophical come-back with his Blue and Brown books of 1933-35.

HOW DID YOUR POSITION CHANGE?

MY SEARCH FOR A PERFECT LANGUAGE LED TO **STALE-MATE**

NOW I FEEL WE MUST SEE LANGUAGE AS A **GAME**

WE LEARN THE RULES BY TRAINING IN CHILDHOOD

IS PHILOSOPHY A GAME THEN?

"The limits of my language are the limits of my reality"

ALL WE CAN DO IS LOOK AT HOW ORDINARY LANGUAGE IS USED

PHILOSOPHY PUTS EVERYTHING BEFORE US & NEITHER EXPLAINS NOR DEDUCES ANYTHING

The meaning of a word is its use

Wittgenstein saw himself as therapist – curing us of the desire to raise metaphysical problems

WHAT IS THE ESSENCE OF BEING, MATE?

Ordinary language philosophy is still with us – one famous living exponent is A J Ayer.

PHILOSOPHICAL SCRABBLE

NOW WHERE? ROUTE 66? I'LL TRY 3, AND GO BACK TO 2

MODERN PHILOSOPHY ROUTE MAP

LANGUAGE

1 Frege
Vienna Circle
Wittgenstein
Russell Whitehead
Gödel
Ordinary Language Philosophy
Ayer etc
SEMIOLOGY Barthes
DE-CONSTRUCTION-ISM

2 Saussure
Linguistics
STRUCTURALISM
Lévi-Strauss
Lacan
Foucault
Althusser
EXIST-ENTIALISM
Sartre etc

3 Brentano
PHENOMEN-OLOGY
Husserl
Heidegger

152

Phenomenology & EXISTENTIALISM

hese inter-related ways of looking at the world are concerned with subjectivity and with a escription of that subjectivity. Phenomenology has been called a "descriptive philosophy of xperience'. **Franz Brentano** (1838-1917) with his descriptive psychology, is seen as the father of he phenomenological school.

WE MUST LOOK PRECISELY AT OUR OWN MENTAL PROCESSES

WASN'T THERE SOMETHING ABOUT **BRACKETS** OR **HINGES**?

Brentano

ALL ASSUMPTIONS ABOUT CAUSES & CONSEQUENCES SHOULD BE ELIMINATED, OR **BRACKETED OUT**

Edmund Husserl — (1859 – 1938) — set out the basic method of phenomenology in his *Logical Investigations*.

STICK TO THE FIRST PERSON. KNOWLEDGE OF YOUR OWN CONSCIOUSNESS IS THE ONE SURE THING

WORK OUT PRECISELY WHAT IS **INTRINSIC** TO MENTAL PROCESSES, & THROW OUT THE REST

BRACKETS AGAIN?

EXACTLY – RID YOURSELF OF PRESUPPOSITIONS

Reason RATIONALISM Theory

SO IT'S EMPIRICAL?

NO – THE METHOD **ISN'T** EMPIRICAL. IT AIMS TO TRANSCEND THE ACTUAL OBJECTS; TO FOCUS ON **THE EXPERIENCE ITSELF**

153

BY A PROCESS OF 'REDUCTION' TO WHAT IS VIVIDLY CLEAR, YOU ARRIVE AT THE ESSENCE OF THE EXPERIENCE

THEN WHAT?

THEN YOU LOOK AT THE OBJECTIVE FUNCTIONS OF THE MIND, THE LOGICAL STRUCTURES THAT LED YOU TO THIS ESSENCE

DON'T YOU GET STUCK IN THE FIRST PERSON?

Husserl got over this problem by talking about "transcendental intersubjectivity", which means that my essences and meanings can be shown, by analogy, to resemble yours.

Husserl emphasized the "intentional" object of consciousness. This is the object - not necessarily real or material - which thinking is "aimed" at.

INTENTIONALITY IS THE HALLMARK OF ALL CONSCIOUSNESS

Sociologists in particular took up the phenomenological method. What Husserl was up to became less and less clear as he developed his thought. In the end he seemed to be saying that the "I" was unknowable. This scepticism is a bit of a problem for phenomology. If you can't know "I", whom can you know? No doubt Wittgenstein would have argued that phenomology was a case of a language-game being taken too far. Anyway if Husserl didn't take it too far, Heidegger certainly did.

Heidegger is variously seen as a phenomenologist, an existentialist, a Nazi, a windbag, or a great mind. He certainly welcomed the rise to power of Hitler, and dissociated himself from Husserl because he was a Jew.

Heidegger said he was a phenomenologist, but everyone else said he was the first atheist existentialist. Most people agree, however, that he is very difficult to follow, almost impossible to summarise, and wildly speculative. His method is light years away from the rigorous logic of analytic philosophy.

Martin Heidegger
(1889 – 1976)

154

$ 64,000 QUESTION

CAN YOU SEPARATE HIS POLITICS & HIS PHILOSOPHY?

IN 'BEING & TIME' I ASKED: "WHAT IS THE MEANING OF BEING?"

AND THE ANSWER?

NEVER MIND.. MY MISSION IS TO MAKE EVERYONE ASK

BACK TO THE THINGS THEMSELVES

Heidegger meant going back to the phenomena, but by phenomena he meant those things which appear to consciousness (hence phenomenology). After Dasein has got together with Phenomena, which is like being meets the world, everything goes wrong when The Other appears. Heidegger was trying to find out the truth about being, a "science of being" that would explain existence.

Dasein experiences 'thrown-ness'—it is knocked backwards on discovering its existence messed up by the OTHER. This produces the FALL into inauthenticity or absurdity.

ANGST!

Anxiety and meaninglessness now set in, and Dasein only knows itself through this anxiety...

As in all good philosophy there is a resolution. It comes when Dasein exercises Care towards the world.

155

Heidegger's search for the truth of being influenced everyone including...

Jean-Paul Sartre (1905 - 1980)

The most famous philosopher of the century, **Jean-Paul Sartre** was responsible for developing the ideas of **Husserl** and **Heidegger** into the coherent body of thought known as **existentialism.**

In his novels, plays and political activity, Sartre was concerned with a philosophy of decision, a philosophy of freedom. He wanted to bring philosophy down into the street. His thinking was about a being-in-the-world.

NO, COME ON, TELL ME WHAT YOU MEAN BY 'EXISTENCE PRECEDES ESSENCE'

WELL, SIMPLY THAT THERE IS NOTHING THAT DETERMINES EXISTENCE, LIKE **GOD** OR THE ABSOLUTE SPIRIT..

SO THERE IS NO ESSENCE

AH, SO YOU EXIST **FIRST**, AND **THEN** FIND OUT WHAT THE ESSENCE OF LIFE IS...

QUITE, AND WHAT YOU DISCOVER IS A **VOID** BETWEEN YOURSELF & THE WORLD. THIS IS THE **NOTHINGNESS** THAT PERMEATES EXISTENCE..

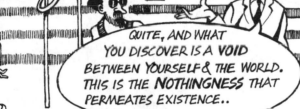

HEIDEGGER TALKED ABOUT THIS AS INAUTHENTICITY

IT HARDLY SEEMS WORTH DISCOVERING

THE TRUTH IS LIKE FINDING YOU ARE FREE, BUT FREE IN A PRISON

SOUNDS LIKE THE ROAD TO FREEDOM LEADS TO THE RIGHT TO FEEL ANGST

157

MEN ALWAYS TRY TO FLEE THE FREEDOM THAT IS THEIR LIFE. THEY THINK, LIKE HEIDEGGER, THAT THERE IS A RESOLUTION

YOU CANNOT CATCH TIME BY THE TAIL

LOOK—I MUST GO, I'M LATE..HONESTLY

The Second World War and the realities of man's inhumanity to man led Sartre to take part in the French Resistance, but also to take more of an interest in Marxism. Sartre didn't deny determination; he thought that man could always make something out of what is made of him. He was always trying to reconcile existentialist freedom with Marxist ideas of collective struggle.

You will by now have noticed the influence of phenomenology on Sartre's work – the idea of intentionality in particular. This was a radical shift in philosophy that said "Let's philosophise about everything, even the everyday things." Along with many others Sartre tried to imagine a new kind of philosophical freedom, one that left nit-picking to the positivitists...

At least with Sartre philosophy was fun, in a French sort of way with plenty of wine, song and ontology.

Sartre did go out on the streets to philosophize, and the debate between existentialism and Marxism dominated French intellectual life until the arrival of structuralism. Sartre, de Beauvoir, and Merleau-Ponty edited *Les Temps Modernes*, a left-wing journal that was central to these debates. Sartre grew more politically active as he grew older, and supported anti-imperialist and revolutionary struggles. He supported Franz Fanon in his attack on colonialism and wrote an introduction to his *The Wretched of the Earth.* In constant debate with his long time companion Simone de Beauvoir he developed a more concrete politics and an understanding of feminism.

Simone de Beauvoir had a great influence on Sartre and was a key figure in Existentialism. She may well however be remembered more for her influence on Feminism. Her seminal book *The Second Sex* (1949) opened up a new wave of feminism that also questioned philosophy and its la[ck] of understanding of the historical and specific nature of women's oppression. From Socrates to Sartre women had been philosophically invisible as a question. This was rather strange as they seemed to constitute rather a large proportion of humankind. Popping the question of "what is woman?" led philosophers to get their metaphysical knickers in a twist.

Sartre believed in freedom, the freedom to make decisions, to take existential 'leaps' into the unknown. De Beauvoir's point in *The Second Sex* was that if everyone possessed this freedom how could you explain women's endless oppression? Did they choose it? Or was this potential freedom something of an illusion, particularly for women? Philosophy claimed to have answers fo[r] everything, but hadn't even addressed this question. This really was a major problem that wasn't going to go away. If philosophy constructed women as 'other' in relation to men, and as therefore subservient, then philosophy itself was failing to conceptualize the conditions under which it operated. It was as blind as the men in Plato's cave!

Wittgenstein and Marx had talked about the end of philosophy, oddly enough from quite a similar point of view.

> FANCY ANALYTIC PHILOSOPHERS AGREEING WITH **ME** THAT SCIENCE SUPERSEDES METAPHYSICS, AND THAT THE WHOLE CONCEPTION OF **PHILOSOPHY** IS ANTIQUATED!

> METAPHYSICS IS THE MISUSE OF LANGUAGE— ALL THAT NINETEENTH CENTURY HEGELIAN STUFF IS PHILOSOPHY ON HOLIDAY, OR OUT TO LUNCH. SCIENCE & ORDINARY LANGUAGE IS WHERE IT'S AT.

Marxists etc.

There is a major difference between these conceptions of philosophy, though. Wittgenstein wants philosophy to fix everything up (philosophy as therapy) so that ordinary life and language can go on, with philosophy as a left-over bit of mechanics. Marx wants to overthrow and reconstruct the social basis of philosophy. Because that social basis keeps changing the interpretation of Marx's view of philosophy also keeps changing.

> IF I'D HAD A QUID FOR EVERYONE WHO CALLED THEMSELVES A MARXIST, I COULD HAVE **BOUGHT** A REVOLUTION

> IT DOESN'T PAY TO BE AHEAD OF YOUR TIME, COMRADE

From Lenin to Gorbachev everyone has an interpretation of Marxism. Philosophy has killed it off several times this century, but it still survives.

161

Some Marxists emphasized the dialectical part of materialism, some the revolutionary, and others the economic or scientific. Then there was Structural Marxism and post-Marxist Marxism.

But even **Stalin** found time to philosophise

> SO DID THE PEOPLE HE LOCKED UP OR EXILED

One of the leaders of the German Sparticists who led an attempted revolution in 1919, Rosa Luxemburg was murdered by army officers during an uprising against the Republican government of Germany. She was very critical of Lenin's democratic centralism and his harsh disciplinarian approach to running the party (*his* party). She believed in mass action and workers' soviets, but the tough boys of Leninist large-scale organisation ignored her. She may be chuckling in her grave over recent events in Leningrad, now re-named St. Petersburg.

WHICH WILL GROW, & WHICH WILL NOT?

Rosa **Luxemburg**

George Lukacs

(1885-1971)

The Hungarian **Georg Lukacs** is the first major Marxist philosopher of this century.

His *History and Class Consciousness* is one of those milestones about which everybody still argues.

IT'S A BOURGEOIS ATTEMPT TO SMUGGLE HEGEL BACK INTO MARXISM

IT'S A BRILLIANT NEW EXPOSITION OF MARX

I TRIED TO CORRECT THE DISTORTIONS OF 'SCIENTISTIC' MARXISM, & TO REINSTATE THE CATEGORY OF TOTALITY TO THE CENTRAL POSITION IT HELD IN MARX'S WORK

Lukacs came out of a bourgeois culture in crisis and tried to make sense of it through the concept of **totality**, with the proletariat as the subject of history. Some of his critics said this was out-Hegeling Hegel, some said he was a 'romantic anti-capitalist', and a bourgeois humanist as well. In part this was because Lukacs spent so much time talking about literature, culture, and philosophy. Lukacs single-handedly brought Marxism into the mainstream of European culture and launched what we now call 'Western Marxism'.

Lukacs argued, like other philosophers before him, that man was alienated in the world and sought wholeness. For Lukacs this was to be achieved through the historical task of the proletariat, the revolution.

Antonio **Gramsci**
(1891 -1937)

The Italian revolutionary **Antonio Gramsci**, who spent much of his life in a Fascist prison, left a philosophical legacy which is still being fought over. Gramsci's central contribution was to introduce the idea of **hegemony** into Marxist thought. His work was not really known until the 1960's though, and it was only in 1975 that a complete edition of his works was published. Like Lukacs he strongly believed in the organic unity of social life.

I AM PERSUADED THAT ALL HUMAN HISTORICAL ACTIVITY IS **ONE**, THAT THOUGHT IS **ONE**

IS THIS WHY COMRADES TALK OF YOUR 'ABSOLUTE HISTORICISM'?

Benedetto Croce (1866-1952)

THAT'S **YOUR** PHRASE, YOU OLD HEGELIAN. YOU'VE DOMINATED ITALIAN THOUGHT WITH YOUR IDEA THAT PHILOSOPHY & HISTORY ARE ONE

BUT YOU BELIEVE IN THE ORGANIC UNITY OF ALL THOUGHT & SOCIAL LIFE?

INDEED — AND **SOCIALISM** IS AN **INTEGRAL VISION** OF LIFE. IT HAS A PHILOSOPHY, A MYSTICISM, & A MORALITY

THERE ARE WHISPERS YOU WERE INFLUENCED BY BERGSON & SOREL

I KNOW, BUT I AM CERTAINLY **NOT** A **ROMANTIC VOLUNTARIST,** WHICH IS THE IMPLICATION

This notion of 'hegemony' is an important addition to marxist philosophy, and may even constitute the end of classical marxism. Gramsci argued that a class had to persuade other classes in society to accept its moral, political and cultural values and that pure economic power wasn't sufficient. Thus he made the role of culture and ideas central to an analysis of the historical moment. Intellectuals, common-sense and popular culture were all areas he discussed which had previously been ignored. He even smuggled the individual back into history.

The Frankfurt School

is the name given to the **Institute for Social Research,** which opened in 1924. Their project was to modernize Marxism and understand modernity.

The failure of the revolutionary parties in the West and the success of Fascism led the Frankfurt School to try to understand capitalism's success.

The Angel of History's face is turned towards the past...
Where we perceive a chain of events, he sees a single catastrophe...
A storm irresistibly propels him into the future, while the debris
before him is piled skywards. This storm is what we call progress"

In trying to understand capitalist culture and forms of mass consciousness, the Frankfurt School drew on psychoanalysis and existentialism. They were concerned with æsthetics, modernism and culture rather than economic determinism.

To help them in this task, the **FRANKFURT SCHOOL** felt they needed a wedding between **MARX & FREUD**

The development of **critical theory** was an attempt to come to terms with the dogged survival of capitalism and the rise of an authoritarian society. The Frankfurt School's pessimism about Europe was compounded by what they saw as the 'mass society' of America. **Horkheimer** and **Adorno** extended their analysis to encompass the bureaucratic states of Eastern Europe as well. Their **critical theory** was to be the bulwark against the incorporation of the working classes into totalitarian society. It was a kind of residue of revolutionary thinking that held itself separate from society, a kind of philosophical memory.

DON'T YOU THINK FORGETTING PAST SUFFERING ALLOWS A REPRESSIVE REALITY PRINCIPLE TO OPERATE?

YOU MEAN MODERN SOCIETY OBLITERATES HISTORY & ASSIMILATES PEOPLE INTO A KIND OF MASS CONSCIOUSNESS?

EXACTLY— WHAT I CALL ONE-DIMENSIONAL **MAN**

SO TRUTH TAKES REFUGE IN SMALL GROUPS OF ADMIRABLE MEN

IT IS THE STRANGE FATE OF CERTAIN INDIVIDUALS & CERTAIN ARTS TO HOLD OUT THE POSSIBILITY OF FUTURE TRUTH

167

WE CAN'T BE **WHOLLY** PESSIMISTIC. THERE IS THE RESIDUE OF CRITICALITY, THE AESTHETIC DIMENSION, AND OF COURSE, PHILOSOPHY ITSELF

AFTER THE CATASTROPHES THAT HAVE HAPPENED, & THOSE TO COME, IT IS **FOOLISH** TO SAY THAT A PLAN FOR A **BETTER** WORLD IS MANIFESTED IN HISTORY & UNITES IT

Jürgen Habermas extended critical theory into new spheres when he began his examination of inter-subjective communication. He examined consciousness and the effects of bureaucratic systems on social life in his famous *Theory of Communicative Action (1981)*. His is one of the last philosophical Marxist approaches to understand the totality, much opposed by post-Structuralists.

Habermas attempted no less than a reconstruction of the foundations of Western Marxism. He tried to put back together a totalizing view of the world, drawing on both the Frankfurt school and more traditional notions of reason. Society still had to be thought of as an integrated, if not orderly, whole. However, given the ever increasing complexity of the social formation, and of language and communication, this was not an easy project. Habermas was critical of the older Frankfurt school pessimism about history and social change, but sometimes unclear about how progress would occur. He is pretty comprehensive and difficult in much of what he writes but always interesting and demanding. Habermas develops his positions as he goes along and his interest in inter-subjective communication and its determinations is where he has been at for a while. He talks about a "universal pragmatics" which is the ways in which ordinary practices form linguistic communications. He seems to be trying to reconstruct some kind of rationality in language but always comes up against different forms of constraints. His systems get bigger and bigger and the end point harder to see. Some argue that the old fashioned realities like domination and subordination get lost in the system.

Louis **Althusser**

(1918 - 1990)

Another strand of Marxist philosophy, which intersected with linguistics and structuralism, was that represented by **Louis Althusser**. He developed a highly complex 'scientific' reworking of Marxism that specified the relative autonomy of political, cultural and intellectual practices determined in the 'last instance' by the economic.

WE MUST REJECT HUMANIST MARXISM. UNDERSTAND THE TRULY SCIENTIFIC MARX, & PUT **STRUCTURE** BEFORE THE INDIVIDUAL

CAN YOU BE A STRUCTURALIST, A MARXIST, AND A LENINIST?

I CAN, THOUGH I'M NOT A STRUCTURALIST AT ALL

WHAT'S YOUR LINE THEN, COMRADE?

THERE ARE **TWO** MARXES – THE EARLY **HUMANIST**, & THE LATER **SCIENTIST**

WHAT SEPARATES THEM?

AN EPISTEMOLOGICAL BREAK, OF COURSE – A PARADIGM SHIFT, A TRANSFORMATION OF THE PROBLEMATICAL

SOUNDS NASTY.. WHAT'S THAT?

THE EARLY MARX SUFFERED FROM BOURGEOIS DELUSIONS. THEN **WHOOMPH!** HE HIT ON THE COMPLEX STRUCTURAL THEORY OF **CAPITAL**, AND ALL WAS CHANGED

LIKE SAUL ON THE ROAD TO DAMASCUS?

ZUT! YOU PRE-SCIENTIFIC THINKERS UNDERSTAND **NOTHING!**

169

AND IDEOLOGY IS 'AN IMAGINARY RELATION TO THE REAL'— IT INTERPOLATES PEOPLE AS CONCRETE SUBJECTS IN CONCRETE POSITIONS

LIKE MAFIA VICTIMS?

THE UNCONSCIOUS FUNCTION OF IDEOLOGY IS PRECISELY TO STRUCTURE THE INDIVIDUAL'S DEVELOPMENT

SO YOU ARE A STRUCTURALIST?

I AM FOR MARX AND FOR A RE-READING OF 'CAPITAL'

HISTORY IS A PROCESS WITHOUT A SUBJECT

AND PHILOSOPHY IS CLASS STRUGGLE AT THE LEVEL OF THEORY, & I'M NIKITA KRUSCHEV

I DON'T KNOW ABOUT YOU—BUT I'M LOST ... COULDN'T WE HAVE SIGN-POSTS?

Route 2
(see page 150)

Structuralism's roots are in the linguistic philosophy of **Saussure**, someone whose work was mostly ignored until the 50s and 60s. He first conceived the notion of looking at the structure of language, rather than how logic operated.

Ferdinand de Saussure
(1857 – 1913)

His abstract model of linguistic structure, his notion of the 'sign' and of language as a system, was taken up and developed into a full-blown science of signs by others. It all began with his posthumous and rather obscure *Cours de Linguistique Generale*.

Langue

RULES of CHESS

Parole

"Think of CHESS. The rules exist only in the abstract, but their embodiment is in a particular, specific game... The game is played by the rules, but isn't the rules"

YOU UNDERSTAND? GOOD. NOW I WANT YOU TO IMAGINE THE WHOLE STRUCTURE OF LANGUAGE AT ANY SPECIFIC MOMENT, FIXED LIKE A SNAPSHOT

AND THAT'S THE SYNCHRONIC AS OPPOSED TO THE DIACHRONIC?

RIGHT. THE EXISTING STRUCTURE OF A LANGUAGE SYSTEM AS OPPOSED TO ITS HISTORICAL GROWTH

WHAT ABOUT SIGNS?

RIGHT. LANGUAGE IS A SYSTEM OF SIGNS THAT EXPRESS IDEAS, SO IT IS COMPARABLE TO THE SYSTEM OF WRITING, TO THE ALPHABET OF DEAF-MUTES, TO SYMBOLIC RITUALS, & TO MILITARY SIGNALS

173

WHAT'S THAT LAST ONE MEAN?

IN LINGUISTICS IT MEANS THAT THE **WORD,** THE **SOUND-IMAGE,** & THE **CONCEPT,** THE **IDEA,** ARE ARBITRARILY RELATED

DOG

SIGNIFIER

SIGNIFIED

There is no natural relationship between the signifier and the signified. 'Dog' doesn't mean 'dog' because it conveys the natural dogginess of dogs. It is the relations between different elements of **language** which constitute the sign 'dog'.

THE POINT BEING THAT ONLY **THE SYSTEM** GIVES SIGNS THEIR MEANING

WHERE THERE IS A **SIGN** THERE IS A SYSTEM

LINGUISTICS is the model for **SEMIOLOGY**

SEMIOLOGY is the model for **STRUCTURALISM**

174

(b1908 -   )

Claude **Lévi-Strauss** was the key figure in rediscovering structural linguistics and applying it to culture as a whole. As an anthropologist, he looked at different cultures and analysed their structural similarities.

SINCE LANGUAGE IS MAN'S DISTINCTIVE FEATURE, IT IS ALSO THE **PROTOTYPE** OF CULTURAL PHENOMENA

IF YOU SPEAK OF **MAN**, YOU SPEAK OF **LANGUAGE**, AND IF YOU SPEAK OF LANGUAGE, YOU SPEAK OF **SOCIETY**

WHAT'S THAT MEAN IN PRACTICE?

.. THAT I EXAMINE PRIMITIVE SOCIETIES TO SEE HOW THEIR CULTURE EXPRESSES CERTAIN SYSTEMS OR SETS OF RULES – THE **STRUCTURE** OF THEIR CULTURE

WHAT DOES THAT THROW UP?

THE SYMBOLIC SYSTEMS OF MYTH THROUGH WHICH PEOPLE LIVE & MAKE SENSE OF THE WORLD OR, I SHOULD SAY, HOW MYTHS THINK IN MEN, UNBEKNOWN TO THEM

SO STRUCTURE IS DOMINANT?

EXACTLY. IT EXPRESSES THE BASIC UNCONSCIOUS STRUCTURES OF THE MIND – THE BINARY OPPOSITIONS THAT UNDERLIE THE WAYS MAN CATEGORISES THE WORLD

175

What Levi-Strauss was getting at was the way in which culture could be seen as a 'signifying system', like language itself. Structuralists, or semioticians, looked below the surface meaning o things (the 'parole') to discover the hidden signifying systems (the 'langue'). Thus all philosophica problems became problems of analysing systems of signs that structured the worlds man lived in. Most analytic philosophers, particularly English and American ones, thought this was all metaphysical tosh and not worth bothering with.

STRUCTURE RULES O.K

Structuralism was anti-humanist and anti-existentialist. For structuralists it was not man who created meaning through language but language which speaks man. The free will debate of humanist philosophy was negated by a concept of a system that wrote people in pre-determined scripts. Everything is fixed at the level of the system, not the individual expressing what they may think are rational independent thoughts. In other words language constitutes reality for us rather than our creating reality through our use of language. Reality becomes the Prison House of Language.

Lacan said we acquire culture as we learn language. Who we are becomes a question of the person who enters into the structures of language. The unconscious part of us is another structure of language.

What started as a theoretical method for understanding language spread quickly during the 1960's and 70's to become an all-embracing philosophy. In literary studies **Roland Barthes** looked at the systems of signification which constituted literature and then at popular culture in *Mythologies*. In psychoanalysis **Lacan** performed a structuralist reading of **Freud** that was then incorporated into the structuralist project. Everything it seemed, even the unconscious, was structured like a language. God, man, religion, myth and philosophy were dead, but not, it seemed, patriarchy.

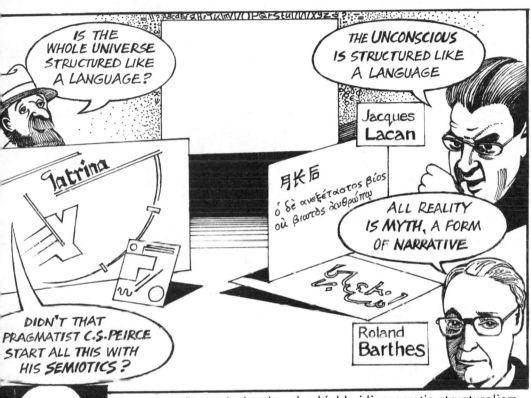

Foucault developed a highly idiosyncratic structuralism, which probably became a post-structuralism, in which he looks at the way in which 'power' operates through complex social structures. He was always concerned with how the knowing subject was constructed, with the discourses of institutions that structured social life and hence the subject. Foucault looks at the forms of knowledge that operate in and through institutions and at their historical development. He recognises that knowledge, truth, power and sexuality are ideas that can change radically, despite setting them in a structured context. This contradictory approach runs throughout Foucault's work. In his rejection of the idea of totalizing theories Foucault can be seen as a post-Structuralist.

Like many overarching philosophical systems structuralism seemed to promise everything and yet not quite to deliver. Everything became so pre-determined that it was hard to find a space for philosophical movement. The attack on the notion of the fixity of the sign, and on grand theories, became known as post-structuralism.

Jacques Derrida was one of the first to blow up structuralism's pretensions to have answered all existing questions. Instead of building structures Derrida set out to 'deconstruct' texts and language. Nothing, it seemed, was as solid as structuralists had imagined. Hidden structures that actually determined the nature of things were only metaphysical constructs as far as Derrida was concerned. To look for a 'science of signs' was to be as rationalistic as Descartes with his dual functioning clocks. Derrida exploded the notion that the sign was fixed by the speaking subject and pointed to the endlessly deferred play of meaning in language.

Fundamentally post-structuralists rejected the basic dualism inherent in structuralist thought and the oppositions like conscious and unconscious, surface and depth on which it operated. **Deconstructionism** aimed to destabilize the myth of fixed meaning and to highlight the irreducible excess of language, the endless play that undermined all texts and all unitary systems. If it sounds a bit like anything goes, then that may be because everybody over-emphasizes the reaction to structuralism. **Habermas** says that post-structuralism falls into linguistic nihilism, making all philosophical statements worthless before you begin. His *Philosophical Discourse of Modernity (1985)* is a good guide to all this. Where it all leaves philosophy. except as a history of illusion, is anybody's guess.

Derrida and others have taken the criticism of structuralist ideas further and have said that all notions of producing philosophical 'truths' are mistaken, misguided and bewildering. Like Foucault, Derrida thinks about the way concepts have been used historically, and how philosophy pretends that there are absolute truths which turn out to be nothing of the sort. This unmasking of the pretensions of philosophy is terribly scandalous and sends traditional philosophers running for their logical principles. If the 'subject' is dead, or has gone missing, and if Western philosophy is based on metaphysical systems which privilege a meaning that is an illusion of presence, then the whole show is nothing but jiggery-pokery. (Jiggery-pokery is an ancient nomadic term for doing things with words). Derrida says that epistemological terms and metaphysical terms are based on binary oppositions that suppress certain terms and privilege others - like "male" and "female". Rather than telling truth philosophy constructs meaning by suppressing, excluding, or marginalizing other terms. He sets out to 'deconstruct' the history of philosophy in order to see what was repressed, hidden or marginalized.

Feminism often takes up this position in relation to thinking about how masculine philosophy has precisely repressed what it means to be "woman", or other. If you look at the things that male philosophers have said, or more importantly not said, then you can see what Derrida is getting at.

There are many strands of post-structuralism (and post-modernism) including people like Baudrillard, Lyotard, Spivak, Kristeva, the Queen and many others. Post-structuralism is, philosophically speaking, a broad church, but no one agrees on where the walls are, or even whether they exist. Apart from dismissing the whole of Western philosophy since Plato's grandfather, calling it rationalistic rubbish, post-structuralism isn't as radical as it sounds. It is however very relevant in thinking about the peculiarities of the modern world, where good old-fashioned cause and effect, truth and falsehood, right and wrong, have gone the same way as the horse drawn cart. Philosophical rightness is now seen as part of a discourse of dominance exercised by Euro-centric males over subordinated groups, like women, blacks, gays, and the Third World as a whole. Post-structuralism opens up the possibility of talking about how knowledge and power go hand in hand; the only question is where they walk to.

OBJECTIVITY IS MALE SUBJECTIVITY

FEMINISM, PHILOSOPHY, AND THE END OF RATIONALISM

In exposing the 'mask of masculinity' that philosophy wears feminism has helped to undermine the certainties that philosophy often aspired to. The grand projects and absolute truths of philosophy have been crumbling away over the last thirty years. The very idea of absolute 'truth', which the early Greeks were searching for, is under attack from many sides. Intelligent computers, post-structuralism,deconstructionism and critiques of the idea of Enlightenment rationalism are all undermining the aspirations of philosophy to provide answers to everything. Some feminists argue that a whole new language, a women's language, must be invented in which to rethink the whole of philosophy. It can be asked "Where has philosophy and science got us to at the moment?" and the answer seems to be in a huge environmental and political mess. Perhaps philosophy has been reduced to personal ethics or the search for small forms of valid knowledge. You pay your money and pick your language game. Ask your computer what a question is. Is this a mouse or an artificially intelligent life form? Is this the last page?

I'M TIRED AFTER READING ALL THAT

IT MAKES YOU THINK, DOESN'T IT?

I CAN'T REMEMBER IF PHILOSOPHERS SORTED OUT ALL THE QUESTIONS

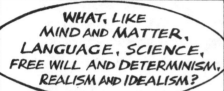

WHAT, LIKE MIND AND MATTER, LANGUAGE, SCIENCE, FREE WILL AND DETERMINISM, REALISM AND IDEALISM?

THOSE WERE THE ONES I HAD IN MIND, OR AT LEAST I THOUGHT I HAD IN MIND

WELL, IF YOU'RE NOT GOD, BUT JUST A RATIONALISTIC MALE THEN YOU PROBABLY THINK WESTERN PHILOSOPHY HAS SOLVED MOST PROBLEMS

I MIGHT BE A POST-STRUCTURALIST NEW MAN

WHAT'S THAT?

WELL, SPEAKING PHILOSOPHICALLY

WHAT'S PHILOSOPHY?

HEY! THAT'S WHERE I CAME IN!

Bibliography

Introductory

Central Questions of Philosophy. A.J.Ayer. 1976.
Philosophy. Brenda Almond. Penguin. 1988.
History of Ancient Philosophy. Bogomolov. 1985.
A History of Philosophy. F.C.Copleston. 1985.
An Invitation to Philosophy. M. Hollis. 1985.
What Philosophy Is. Anthony O'Hear. Penguin. 1985.
The Great Philosophers. B. Magee.
A Hundred Years of Philosophy. J. Passmore. 1968.
Philosophy Made Simple. Popkin & Stroll. Made Simple Books. 1986.
The Problems of Philosophy. Bertrand Russell. 1961.
History of Western Philosophy. Bertrand Russell. 1959
A Short History of Modern Philosophy. R. Scruton. 1984.
Philosophy in the Open. G. Vesey (ed.). 1974.
The Concise Encyclopedia of Western Philosophy. Urmson & Ree. 1989

Advanced & General

Ethics. Aristotle. 1976.
Politics. Aristotle. 1981.
Confessions. Augustine. 1961.
Three Dialogues. G. Berkeley (Philosophical Works) 1975.
The Owl of Minerva: Philosophers on Philosophy. C.J. Bontempo and S.J. Odell (eds.). 1975
Early Greek Philosophy. J.Burnet. 1945.
On the Nature of the Gods. Cicero. 1972
Gender and Power. R.W. Connell. 1987.
Beyond God the Father. M. Daly. 1986
On Grammatology. J. Derrida. 1976.
Thinking about Thinking. A. Flew. 1985
Feminist Philosophers. J. Grimshaw. 1986.
The Philosophical Discourse of Modernity. J. Habermas. 1988.
A Treatise on Human Nature. D. Hume. 1985.

Ibn-Khaldun. trans. Issaawi. 1951

Women in Western Political Philosophy. E. Kennedy & S. Mendus. 1987.

The Revolution in Poetic Language. J. Kristeva. 1984.

The Man of Reason. G. Lloyd. 1984.

A Short History of Ethics. A Macintyre. 1967.

After Philosophy: End or Transformation. McCarthy, Bowman & Baynes (eds.). 1987.

Anarchy, State & Utopia. R. Nozick. 1974.

A Critical History of Western Philosophy. D.J. O'Conner. 1964.

Radical Philosophy Reader. R. Osborne & R. Edgley. 1985.

Reason, Truth & History. H. Putman. 1981.

A Theory of Justice. J. Rawls. 1971.

Political Thought from Plato to NATO. B. Redhead (ed.). 1984.

Philosophy and the Mirror of Nature. R. Rorty. 1980.

The Social Contract. J.J.Rousseau (trans. G.D. Cole). 1973.

The Computer Revolution in Philosophy. A. Sloman. 1978.

AIDS, Philosophy & Beyond. J.W.Smith. 1991.

Structuralism and Since. J. Sturrock. 1958.

The Anti-Philosophers. R.J.White. 1970.

Tractatus Logico-Philosophicus. L. Wittggenstein. 1921.

INDEX